A READER'S COMPANION III

3,500 WORDS AND PHRASES
AVID READERS SHOULD KNOW

John L. Bowman

A Reader's Companion III

ISBN 978-0-578-55798-4

Any people depicted in stock imagery are models,
which are being used for illustrative purposes only.
Because of the dynamic nature of the Internet, any web addresses
or links contained in this book may have changed
since publication and may no longer be valid.
The views expressed in this work are solely those of the author.

This book was printed on acid-free paper.

This book is dedicated to all the logophiles of the world.

The cover is the painting *The Waterseller of Seville* by Velázquez. Water selling was a common trade for the lower classes in Velázquez's Seville. It is a striking painting that represents many aspects of his painting style. The theme is still and calm, and the water seller has a pensive face battered by exposure to the sun and deeply scarred with wrinkles of age that speak of long years of experience. It reflects Velázquez's respect for the poor. Perhaps above all it is his typical precise depiction of the small details of reality.

ACKNOWLEDGEMENTS

The 3,500 words and phrases in this book are taken from a variety of sources: wordbooks, dictionaries, encyclopedias, word of mouth, books, various readings, my computer and conversations. They are among the most commonly recurring. Note however when the meaning of a word or phrase could not be found in the dictionary I sometimes surmised its definition from its roots.

I would like to thank my longtime trusted editor Kat Banks for editing this book.

INTRODUCTION

A Reader's Companion III: 3,500 words and phrases avid readers should know is the third in my trilogy of books on words. The first edition was published in 2007 and this one in 2019, a span of twelve years during which I looked up the definition of more than 10,500 words. It was a rewarding effort.

I selected words for these three books for a variety of reasons. The main one was that I simply did not know what a word meant. Also, I sometimes I looked up a word because I read it in a different context and discovered its meaning was not what I thought it was. I usually included words that were similar but had different meanings. In this book, for example, immanent, which means existing within or inherent in something; eminent, which means of superior position, fame or achievement; and imminent, which means about to happen or threatening to happen, are similar. I also often include interesting words like phoneme, which means the smallest speech sound that distinguishes one word from another and carries meaning. There are subtle phonemes, for example, that distinguish immanent, eminent and imminent.

I also include common words with broader meanings like sieve, which we usually think is a utensil but in fact is any device used for separating wanted material from unwanted material. I like words with interesting contrasts like pecunious, which means having money, moneyed or wealthy and impecunious, which means the opposite or having little or no money, or to be poor. Other examples are astronaut, which is one trained to travel and perform tasks in space, as opposed to intranaut, which is an individual who explores or reflects on his or her own mind in search of meaning, and pertinacity, which means to be resolute in purpose or determined, versus impertinent, which means to be brash.

I sometimes include familiar words because they are from a root word with a lesser known meaning. Illicit, for example, which means illegal, derives from the word licit, which means legal. Finally, I included words describing different relations. In marriage, for example we all know monogamy, which means being married to only one person at a time, and perhaps polygamy, which means having more than one spouse at the same time. But there is also polyandry, or having more than one husband at the same time; exogamy, which is the custom of marrying outside one's social group; and endogamy, which is the custom of marrying a member of one's social group.

There are a few final housecleaning comments. I am not a lexicographer, and this is not a scholarly book but rather a brief summary of the definitions of many words and phrases I have encountered in context. Most definitions are brief, abbreviated and in incomplete sentences. The definitions are not in correct literary or scholastic form. I usually exclude etymology, pronunciation and root meanings. I occasionally give synonyms and antonyms. I usually ignore the obvious meaning of a word and give only the lesser known ones. When words have more than one meaning, I separate them with a semicolon. When words defining one meaning of a word are similar, they are separated by a comma. I occasionally include some comments of my own and expand on a word's meaning. Also, I often add comparison words with cf. (Latin for confer, compare) that have similar or dissimilar meanings or create an interesting contrast. The comparison words can be found elsewhere in this book. Finally, many of the words are proper nouns for places and persons as well as Latin and literary words and phrases.

In conclusion, I must apologize because there are some words in this book that were in the previous books. Sometimes I found a better definition or a new meaning, or I just forgot the word.

A

A cappella—unaccompanied by musical instruments; by voices only

A fortiori—Latin for an even stronger reason, with more reason

A posse ad esse—Latin for "from possibility to actuality"

A tergo—Latin for "from behind"a

Á tout prix—French for "at all costs"

Ab aeterno—Latin meaning from an infinitely remote point of time in the past

Ab initio—Latin for "from the beginning"

Ab ovo—Latin for "from the egg" or metaphorically from the very beginning

Abase—to belittle or degrade somebody; to behave in such a way that lowers your dignity or self-esteem

Abate—to nullify

Abatis—a defensive obstacle formed by felled trees with sharp-ened branches facing the enemy

Abattoirs—a slaughterhouse

Abide—to tolerate something, to endure or withstand something; to live in a place; to wait for something or somebody

Abject—miserable with no hope; excessively humble; despicable or contemptible

Abjuration—to give up a previously held belief, especially formally or solemnly; to abstain from, reject or avoid something, to deny yourself something

Abjure—to solemnly renounce a belief, cause or claim

Ablution—the act of washing oneself, especially in a religious ritual; the ritual of cleansing a priest's hands or body during a religious ceremony

Abnegation—to give up or renounce something

Abominate—to loathe, hate, abhor or detest someone

Aborning—a native dialect of the early twentieth century in the rural South

Abortifacient—a drug or device that causes abortion

Abrogate—to repeal, annul or cancel something

Abscissae—in a system of coordinates, the x-coordinate, the distance from a point to the vertical or y-axis measured parallel to the horizontal or x-axis

Abstemious—to act in moderation, especially in eating and drinking

Abstersion—the action or process of cleansing, the act of wiping clean, purging

Abstruse—something incomprehensible, unintelligible, not clear

Abus du droit—French meaning "abuse of right," e.g. a person can be held accountable for any harm they cause that they had no right to cause

Acanthus—a spiny-leafed bush or perennial plant with white and purple flowers native to the Mediterranean; a design characteristic of the capital of a Corinthian column representing acanthus leaves

Accidia—sloth, laziness (one of the seven deadly sins)

Accompt—to account

Accoucheur—a man who works as a midwife or obstetrician

Accoutred—to clothe or equip in something noticeable or impressive

Acerbic—to be sour, bitter or harsh

Acoustic shadow—a place where sounds die due to coming from a certain direction on a given day and the presence of dense material

Acronym—a word formed from the initial letters of a group of words, e.g. NATO stands for North Atlantic Treaty Organization

Acrophonic—the use of a logogram as a phonetic symbol; cf. logogram

Acrostic—a poem, word puzzle or other composition in which certain letters in each line form a word or words, for example the first letters of the sentences in the poem "roses are red/oranges yummy/sugar's sweet and/elixir in my tummy" spells "rose"

Acte gratuite—Latin meaning an impulsive act lacking motive

Actus purus—from scholastic philosophy, "pure act" intended to express the absolute perfection of God

Acute—in some languages a mark placed above a letter to show that it is pronounced in a specific way such as "é" in French; cf. cedilla

Ad acta—Latin meaning not actual any more, to archives

Ad libitum—Latin for "at one's pleasure"; something to be performed in the way the performer chooses

Adamant—a legendary extremely hard stone sometimes thought to be a diamond or lodestone

Adano—a Sicilian city made famous by John Hersey's novel *A Bell for Adano* about an Italian-American officer who helped the citizens find a replacement bell after the Fascists melted the original down for rifle barrels

Adaze—in ancient times, an edge tool used for smoothing or carving wood in woodworking

Adjure—to urge or request someone solemnly or earnestly to do something

Adjuvant—a drug added to another drug to enhance its medical effectiveness; something that helps or assists

Adlatus—Latin meaning carried forth or delivered

Adrenochrome—a naturally occurring substance that reduces the permeability of blood vessels used to control bleeding

Adspice—Latin meaning examine the present; cf. respice, prospice

Adumbrate—to sketchily indicate something, to foreshadow, to give a warning of something to come

Adverbial—relating to or functioning as an adverb

Advertence—to call attention or make reference to something; cf. inadvertence

Adynamia—lack of strength or vigor due to a pathological condition like sclerosis lobe lesions

Adze—a tool similar to an axe with an arched blade at right angles to the handle used for shaping wood

Aegis—the sponsorship or patronage of something or someone

Aegisthus—a character in Greek mythology who fought at Troy, had a long time rivalry with his brother, seduced Agamemnon's wife Clytemnestra and was killed by her son Orestes

Aeitology—the study of causes, primarily used in medicine that deals with the causes of illness

Aenigmate—an enigma, riddle; an allegory

Aeolian harp—a musical instrument with strings that sound when wind blows over them; an eerie shimmering sound that floats on the breeze

Aeon—another spelling of eon, or a vast amount of time, a length of time too long to measure

Aere perennius—a monument more lasting than bronze, a quote from Horace claiming that poetry will outlive any man-made monument

Aereal—any extent of space or surface; the dark areas of a painting; the dusty area of a room

Aesop—an ancient Greek fabulist and story teller who wrote *Aesop's Fables*

Aesopian—relating to the characteristics of Aesop or his fables

Aesthetic—pleasing in appearance; sensitive to or appreciating beauty

Aevum—in Scholastic philosophy, the mode of existence experienced by angels and saints in heaven

Affected—exaggerated, pretentious, artificial, unnatural

Afflatus—an impulse of creative power or inspiration, especially in poetry

Afrite—in Arabian mythology the same as afreet, an evil spirit or powerful monster

Agape—open-mouthed, usually due to surprise or wonder; love that is selfless, spiritual and nonsexual, e.g. Christian love; in early Christianity, a communal meal in commemoration of the Last Supper

Agglutination—the clumping of particles; in linguistics when complex words are formed from stringing together morphemes

Agnosticism—the doctrine that God nor the origin of the universe is known or knowable; any doctrine that asserts all knowledge is relative and therefore uncertain; cf. gnostic, gnosis, Gnosticism, agnostic

Agnostic—unknowing, unknown; cf. gnostic, gnosis, Gnosticism, agnosticism

Agonal—pertaining to the process of death or moment of death, due to the notion that dying is a painful process or struggle; agonal respiration is irregular, gasping breaths often seen during cardiac arrest

Agranulocytosis—a blood disease characterized by a decrease in white blood cells and lesions of the throat, gastrointestinal tract and skin that is sometimes fatal

Agroikia—a form of comedy that includes a rustic country bumpkin who is easily deceived

Ague—a feverish condition with alternating hot, cold and sweating stages, especially as a symptom of malaria; a fever of shivering fit

Aiguillette—decorative cord worn on the shoulder of military uniforms

Aion—a Hellenistic deity associated with unbounded time and the universe; cf. Chronos

Aitch—the letter "h" or its sound

Akatastasia—Greek for a state of disorder, disturbance or confusion

Al pari di—Italian for "as an equal"

Alack—to express regret

Alacrity—to do something with cheerful and eager readiness

Alarum—same as alarm, to warn, to cause to fear

Alaunt—a breed of dog used for guarding

Albatross—another term for double eagle in golf

Aldermanic—another spelling of ealdorman, a man who is a member of a legislating body in the United States and England

Alembic—an apparatus formerly used in distillation

Alençon—a delicate needlepoint lace

Alexandrine—a line of poetic meter comprising twelve syllables

Aliment—something that feeds, sustains or supports something else

Aliquot—a number or quantity that will divide another number or quality without leaving a remainder, to divide into something exactly

Alliteration—the repetition of a sound or letter in two or more words such as "bewitched and bewildered"

Allopathic—the treatment of disease by conventional means, i.e. with drugs having the opposite effects of the symptoms; cf. homeopathy

Almeira—an ancient Roman city in southeast Spain on the Mediterranean Sea and capital of its province of the same name that suffered many sieges under Christian domination in the fifteenth century

Almoner—historically, somebody who gives to the needy, especially on behalf of the church; in the United Kingdom, a social worker at a hospital

Alnaschar—a person given to unrealistic dreams or expectations, especially for wealth or success

Aloes—a bitter-tasting aloe leaf extract used as a laxative; the fragrant wood of the eaglewood tree from which a resin is obtained, resinous wood

Alpaca—a longhaired South American animal related to the llama and similar in appearance; wool or cloth made from the long shaggy hair of the alpaca, e.g. the alpaca coat

Alsatian—same as a German shepherd dog

Alterity—a philosophical and anthropological term meaning "otherness," strictly in the sense of the other of two

Altiplano—the high tableland of central South America

Amanuensis—a secretary

Amaranth—a plant with leafy vegetables and long drooping heads grown for ornament and sometimes as a grain crop; according to legend, a flower that never fades; a synthetic red food dye

Amative—amorous, an inclination toward love, especially sexual love

Ambracia—in Greek mythology an Oeachalian princess and daughter of Melaneus

Amenorrhea—the absence of a menstrual period in a woman of reproductive age

Amfortas's wound—a wound that caused Amfortas suffering and shame that never healed on its own; a wound that never heals

Amir—same as emir or in Islamic countries an independent ruler, commander or governor; the title for a descendant of the prophet Muhammad

Ammonal—a high explosive consisting of powered aluminum, ammonium nitrate and TNT

Ammoniacal—containing or resembling ammonia

Amnion—an inner membrane enclosing the embryo of a mammal and its surrounding fluid

Amor patrioe—Latin meaning love of one's country

Amoroso—something performed in a gentle, loving way; a sweet dark sherry

Amorous—strongly moved by love, especially sexual love

Amorphism—lack of shape, form, structure or classifying features

Amour courtois—an idealized and often illicit form of love celebrated in the Middle Ages in which a knight devotes himself to a married noblewoman who feigns indifference to preserve her reputation; an illicit, secret and demeaning love affair

Amoureuse—French meaning to be in love

Amour-propre—French for self-love, self-esteem; Jean-Jacque Rousseau contrasted esteem based on that which comes from others' opinion of us with amour de soi, which also means self-love but does not depend on others' opinions

Amphictyony—ancient Greek religious alliances that shared responsibility for shrines and temples

Amphora—in ancient Greece and Rome, a jar with a narrow neck and two handles used for holding oil or wine

Ampoule—a sealed glass container that holds medication to be injected

Ampule—a small sealed container that holds medicine to be injected

Anael—an angel messenger of Venus in Cabalism

Anagogical—from Greek to climb or ascent upwards, a mystical interpretation such as in religious writings intended to reveal a hidden, spiritual meaning

Anagram—a word formed from the rearrangement of the letters of another word, e.g. vile is an anagram of evil

Anagrammatic—a word, phrase or name formed by rearranging the letters of another in the form of an anagram, as in "angel" is anagrammatic of "glean"

Analeptic—a medication that is restorative or invigorating, a stimulant

Anamnesis—in Platonic philosophy, the remembering of things from a supposed previous existence; the theory that knowledge is recollection

Anapestic—a metrical foot of three syllables with stress on the third syllable as in "unconcerned" or two short syllables followed by a long syllable as in "up the hill"

Anaphora—the use of the same word or phrase at the beginning of several lines or verses used for rhetorical effect

Anathema—somebody or something cursed, denounced or excommunicated by religious authority; a forceful curse or denunciation

Anchorite—a person who has retired to a solitary place for a life of religious seclusion, a hermit

Andalusia—a region of southern Spain containing Seville; a pure-bred Spanish horse

Andalusian—an autonomous region of southern Spain containing the cities of Seville and Grenada with a strong Moorish history

Andromache—in Greek mythology, a princess of Troy and wife of Hector who led the Trojan women throughout the Trojan War

Anemometer—an instrument that measures the force and direction of wind

Anemone—a perennial flowering plant of the buttercup family; a flowering plant

Anergic—decreasing immunity or lack of immunity to an antigen

Anglaise—various English dances popular in Europe in the seventeenth and eighteenth centuries

Angora—a rabbit, goat or cat belonging to a breed with long silky fur; wool made from the hair of an Angora goat or rabbit

Aniline—a colorless poisonous oily liquid used in dyes and explosives

Animadversion—a critical comment usually reproaching somebody

Animadvert—to speak out against

Animalcule—a microscopic organism that resembles an animal such as an amoeba that moves about and eats other microbes

Anima—the personification of the feminine nature of a man's unconscious; cf. animus

Animism—the attribution of a soul to plants, inanimate objects and natural phenomena; the belief in a supernatural power that organizes and animates the material world

Animistic—Latin for soul or spirit; the belief that everything has awareness and feelings including rocks and trees and that they can communicate with humans

Animus—to have hostility and antagonism; the personification of the masculine nature of a woman's unconscious; cf. anima

Anise—an aromatic plant with licorice-flavored seeds native to the Mediterranean; same as aniseed, or licorice-flavored seeds used for flavoring

Annate—when the whole of the first year's profits of a benefice is given to the papal treasury

Anneal—to make something stronger through heating; to make something stronger or more resolute such as an opinion, feeling or intention

Annulate—ring-shaped or consisting of rings

Annulosa—a subkingdom of animals that have articulate bodies and ganglia

Annus horribilis—Latin for "a horrible year"; cf. annus mirabilis

Annus mirabilis—Latin for "a wonderful year"; cf. annus horribilis

Anodyne—a pain reliever; something that soothes, comforts or relaxes, hence figuratively a comforting thing

Anomaly—a deviation from the general rule or type

Anomic—from anomie, a breakdown in societal norms with the attendant loss of moral guidance for individuals

Anon—at an unspecified time in the future, another time, as in "I will see you soon"; in a short while, soon

Anonym—an author whose name is not known or given; a name used by somebody to hide their identity, a pseudonym

Anorak—a waterproof jacket, typically with a hood, used in polar regions; a studious or obsessive person with unfashionable and largely solitary interests

Anserine—relating to or resembling a goose; stupid, silly as in an "anserine behavior"

Antaeus—in Greek mythology, a strong Libyan giant with a connection with his mother the earth who forced travelers to wrestle with him

Anta—the thick end of the side of a wall of a Greek temple that forms one side of a porch

Ante rem—prior in reality or existence to particulars, or universals prior to particulars; logically preceding something else; cf. in rem

Antediluvian—from the time before the biblical flood; extremely old-fashioned or outdated; cf. diluvium

Anthracite—a hard shiny black coal that is clean burning, high in carbon content and low in volatile matter

Anthroparion—a tiny man, a kind of homunculus

Anthropomorphic—ascribing human characteristics to gods, animals or other objects

Anthropophagous—somebody who eats human flesh, a cannibal

Anthropos—Greek for human; in Gnosticism the first human being

Antibiotic—a substance that kills bacteria but has no effect against viruses, used as a medication; cf. biotic

Antibody—a protein that fights infections and disease

Antient—obsolete spelling of ancient

Antiepirrhema—in ancient Greek comedy, the continuation of an epirrhema following an antistrophe; cf. epirrhema

Antigen—a substance, usually protein, that stimulates the production of an antibody

Antimony—a brittle metallic toxic crystalline chemical element

Antinomian—a Christian who believes faith and divine grace bring salvation thus it is not necessary to follow established moral laws

Antipathetic—feeling anger, hostility or disgust for something or somebody, feeling a dislike; causing anger or disgust, repulsive

Antipathy—to have an aversion or strong dislike

Antiperistasis—in philosophy, processes whereby one quality heightens the force of another opposing quality, as in the ostensible interaction between thunder and lightning

Antiphlogistic—an older medical term denoting the capacity to prevent or relieve inflammation; an agent that reduces inflammation

Antiphon—a hymn or psalm performed by two groups of singers chanting alternate sections; a short devotional text chanted or sung before or after a psalm; a response or reply; in Christian liturgy, a short sentence sung or recited before or after a psalm or canticle

Antiphrasis—from Greek meaning the opposite word, a figure of speech where a word or phrase is opposite its literal meaning

Antipode—the exact or diametric opposite

Antiquary—a collector or scholar of antiques or antiquities; somebody interested in old objects

Antisepsis—the reduction or elimination of microorganisms that cause disease or decay primarily to prevent infection; cf. asepsis

Antispastic—relieving or preventing spasms, especially of voluntary skeletal muscles

Antistrophe—in ancient Greek tragedy the second part of the ode (after the strophe); cf. strophe, epode

Antithetic—constituting the exact opposite, diametrically opposed; a proposition that is opposed to another, contrasting with an earlier proposition

Antonine—the Antonine Wall was a Roman frontier wall across Scotland from the River Clyde to the Firth of Fourth

Aorist—a verb tense used to express past action in an unqualified way without specifying that action continued or how long it lasted, found primarily in classical Greece

Apadana—in Persian architecture, a large hypostyle (cf. hypostyle) hall such as the great audience hall at Persepolis

Apanage—a gift of land, official position or money given to the younger children of a king or prince

Apelles—a renowned painter in ancient Greece considered the greatest painter of antiquity; a mid–second-century Gnostic Christian destined to bear the palm from all his predecessors and successors

Aperient—a mild laxative

Aphasia—the inability to produce or understand speech due to brain damage

Aphelion— the point of a planet, asteroid or comet at which it is furthest from the sun; cf. perihelion

Aphorism—a concise statement of a general truth

Aphoristic—a succinct statement expressing an opinion or general truth, a pithy saying

Aphtha—a small ulcer occurring in groups in the mouth or on the tongue

Apiculture—the keeping of bees, especially for commercial purposes, beekeeping

Aplomb—to have poise, be self-assured and imperturbable

Apocalypse—a prophetic revelation, especially a cataclysm where good wins over evil; any revelation or prophecy

Apocatastas—the religious belief that in the end everything in existence will be saved and brought into the Kingdom of God

Apocryhon—secret writings, Greek for Jewish and early Christian writings that were meant to impart "secret teachings" or gnosis (knowledge) that could not be publically taught

Apocrypha—a group of early Christian writings not included in the bible; biblical writings of disputed authenticity

Apocryphal—something probably not true but widely believed to be true; erroneous, fictitious; of doubtful authorship or authenticity; in religious context, disagreement about biblical canonicity

Apogee—the high point, climax or summit

Apollo—in classical Greek and Roman mythology, the god of music, truth, prophecy, healing, the sun and light, plague and poetry

Apollonian—relating to the ancient Greek god Apollo; figuratively clarity, harmony and restraint; serenely high-minded, noble and perfect; from Friedrich Nietzsche, embodying the power of critical reason as opposed to creative-intuitive thinking

Apologia pro vita sua—Latin meaning a defense of one's own life, which was John Henry Newman's defense of his religious opinions

Apologue—a fable that is intended to teach a moral lesson, especially with animals or characters

Apophantic—Greek meaning to show, to make known; the term was coined by Aristotle to mean a type of declaratory statement that can determine truth or falsity of a logical proposition, the term is used today in phenomenology

Apophatic—knowledge gained through negation, in religion the belief that God can only be described by the process of negation

Apophthegm—same as apothegm, a terse statement that embodies an important truth, e.g. clogs to clogs in three generations

Apoplectic—to be angry, enraged, furious or seething

Aporetic—confusion in establishing the truth of a proposition, difficulty in establishing truth; tending to doubt, a voice that expresses wonder and perplexity, from the Greek word meaning "to be at a loss"

Aporia—confusion in establishing the truth of a proposition, difficulty in establishing truth

Apostasy—the renunciation of a religious or political belief

Apostate—a person who renounces their faith or party; a renegade or defector

Aposteriorally—located in front or toward the front of a structure, near the front, the opposite of posteriorally

Apostolic—relating to the Apostles

Apostrophe—a rhetorical passage that addresses an imaginary person or inanimate entity

Apostrophize—to address an absent or imaginary person or personified abstraction

Apotheosis—literally, deification, to be divine; figuratively, glorification or a supreme example

Appellation—a name applied to somebody or something

Applesauce—silly nonsense

Apposite—especially well suited to the circumstances, appropriate, apt or relevant

Appresentation—from Husserl, the function of a presentation as motivating the experiential positing of something else as present along with the presented object

Apropos—appropriate in a specific situation, just right; on the subject of, in regard to; by the way, incidentally

Apse—in architecture, a semicircular recess covered with a hemispherical vault or semi-dome, also known as an exedra

Aqua Florida—same as aquamarine or a greenish blue gemstone; a greenish blue color; water, especially when used in the pharmaceutical industry as a solvent

Aquatint—a method of etching a copper plate that produces watercolor-like prints

Arabesque—in ballet a position where the dancer stands on one leg with the other extended back and forth; an ornate, intricate design with curves, leaves, flowers and animal shapes; in music, an ornate style characterized by melodies

Arbalest—a medieval crossbow used to propel missiles

Arbeit—physical or mental effort or activity directed toward the production or accomplishment of something (arbeit mach frei is a German phrase meaning "work sets you free," a slogan that appeared at the entrance of Auschwitz and other Nazi concentration camps)

Arcady—from Greek Arcadia in the central Peloponnese considered a harmonious unspoiled wilderness; an ideal rustic paradise

Arcanum—a secret known only to a select group; a secret of nature formerly sought by alchemists

Arcanum—secrets or mysteries

Archaism—a thing that is very old or old fashioned; an archaic word or style of language or art

Archein—to begin

Archetypal—an original model or prototype, a model on which other things copy; cf. ectypal

Archiepiscopal—relating to an archbishop or archdiocese

Archimandrite—a senior priest or head of a monastery

Archimedean point—a point of reference outside of Earth and humans, an objective point of reference, a universal perspective

Architectonic—relating to architecture or the qualities it requires; relating to the classification of knowledge used in metaphysics

Architrave—in classical architecture, the lowest section of an entablature when it comes in contact with the top of the columns; the decorative strip of wood or plaster forming a frame around a door or window

Archly—knowing playfulness, mischief and shared humor; the greatest, especially most hostile

Archon—in ancient Greece, one of nine Athenian magistrates

Areopagus—a prominent rock outcropping located northwest of the Acropolis in Athens known as Ares Rock in English used in classical times as a court to try cases of homicide

Aretino—Pietro Aretino was a sixteenth-century Italian writer and satirist best known for his literary attacks on the wealthy and powerful; figuratively, a satire of the wealthy and powerful

Argosy—a large, richly laden merchant ship or fleet of such ships

Argot—jargon, the idiom of a particular class of people

Argyrol—a mild silver protein anti-infective compound used to treat some infections that was commonly used for most infections before antibiotics

Ariadne's thread—in mythology, Ariadne used a ball of thread that she unrolled in the Minotaur's labyrinth thus allowing her to find her way out; figuratively, to solve a complex problem with multiple apparent means of proceeding, such as a physical maze, long puzzle or ethical dilemma, through exhaustive application of logic to all available routes; cf. Ariadne

Ariadne—in Greek mythology, a Cretan princess associated with mazes and labyrinths because of her involvement in the myths of the Minotaur and Theseus; cf. Ariadne's Thread

Arietta—an English word meaning melody; used generally as a girl's name

Aristarchus—Aristarchus of Samos (c. 310–c. 230 BCE) was a Greek astronomer and mathematician who presented the first known heliocentric model that placed the sun at the center of the universe and Earth revolving around it

Armamentarium—the complete range of equipment, medications and techniques available to a medical practitioner

Armillary—a model of objects in the sky consisting of a spherical framework of rings, centered on Earth or the sun along with astronomically important features

Armoire—a tall cupboard or wardrobe usually ornately decorated originally used to store weapons

Armorial—relating to or decorated with a coat of arms

Arpent—a French unit of land measure, about 0.85 acres

Arrack—alcoholic liquor typically distilled from coconut palm or rice

Arrant—a word used to intensify the quality of a person or thing, e.g. "Hitler was an errant despot"

Array—in law, a panel of jurors

Arrhethon—a Greek word referring to Arrhetos, a Gnostic, meaning ineffable, unspeakable or in mystical philosophy not to be divulged; something considered so holy or sacred that it is improper to divulge it to the public

Arriviste—somebody who has become socially prominent and is regarded as an upstart, a social climber

Arrogate—to claim something as one's own without right

Ars longa, vita brevis—Latin for "art is long, life is short"

Artful—to be crafty, deceitful and cunning; cf. artless

Artisanal—a skilled craftsman

Artless—to be free from deceit, guile and cunning; cf. artful

Asafetida—a bitter brownish acrid-smelling plant resin; a plant of the parsley family that produces asafetida

Asafoetida—a bitter brownish acrid-smelling plant resin used in Asian cuisine

Ascribe—to designate a cause of something; to designate something as a characteristic of a person or group; cf. attribution

Asepsis—a condition where no disease-causing microorganisms are present; the elimination of germs; cf. antisepsis

Askaris—a solider or police officer in Islamic countries of eastern Africa

Askesis—strict self-discipline or self-control as for religious or medical purposes

Aspergillum—an implement for sprinkling holy water

Asperity—harshness or severity of manner or tone; something hard to bear due to its harshness or severity; the roughness of a surface

Aspersion—damaging assertions, slandering or vilification

Asphaltus—obsolete term for asphalt

Aspic—a dish made of gelatin made from meat stock or consommé, a jelly made from meat or fish often used to form a mold of fish, meat, eggs or vegetables

Assegaiing—to pierce with an assegai; cf. assegais

Assegais—a slender hardwood spear with an iron tip, used especially by the Zulu peoples of Africa; cf. assegaiing

Asseverate—to state something earnestly and solemnly

Assiduous—perseverance, diligence and effort

Assize—in England, a court that sat at intervals in counties to administer civil and criminal law

Assonantal—the similarity of two or more vowel sounds or repetition of consonant sounds, especially in a poem

Assuage—to sooth and relieve

Asthenic—physical weakness; having a slender or lightly muscled body, of slender build; cf. sthenic

Astragal—a narrow convex molding often in the form of beads; a small convex molding attached to double doors to prevent drafts

Astrakhan cap—a wedge shaped hat covered in seal skin or synthetic fur; fur fabric made from the curly dark fleece of lambs from Astrakhan, southern Russia

Astronaut—one trained to travel and perform tasks in space; an Asian immigrant whose family settled in the West but travels often to Asia to work; cf. intranaut

Asymptote—in mathematics, a line that a graph approaches but does not intersect

Atabrine—an early anti-malarial drug

Ataraxia—freedom from worry, peace of mind

Atavistic—the recurrence of a genetic feature that has been absent for generations; to exhibit characteristics of forbearers or of primitive cultures; displaying impulsive behavior repressed by society

Atë—the Greek goddess of mischief, delusion, ruin and folly; the action of a hero that brings their downfall due to hubris

Athwart—to be across or crosswise over something; to oppose or obstruct something

Atrabilious—tending to feel sad or gloomy; inclined to peevishness and irritability, peevish

Attenuate—to weaken something, to reduce in intensity or value; cf. enervate

Attic salt—refined, delicate wit, also known as attic wit

Attic—elegantly succinct or drily witty

Attitudinizing—to consciously strike exaggerated or unspontaneous poses or adopt opinions for effect, to consciously adopt postures or opinions

Attribution—to ascribe something to something or somebody; cf. ascribe

Aubade—a song or poem celebrating dawn

Auditory—relating to the organs of hearing or process of hearing

Auge—in Greek mythology, the daughter of Aleus and Neaera and priestess of Athena who bore the hero Telephus

Aught—anything at all

Augur—to foreshadow

Aulnager—an inspector of the quality and measurement of woolen cloth, also spelled alnager

Aurea Catena—the "Golden Chain" in alchemy is a series of great wise men that links Earth with heaven (definition from Carl Jung's *Memories, Dreams, Reflections*)

Aureole—a circle of light or brightness surrounding something, especially as depicted in art around the head or body of a person represented as holy

Auroch—Europe's last wild bison

Auspice—a sign or token for the future, especially a happy or promising one

Austral—southernmost, of the Southern hemisphere, e.g. Australia is an austral continent

Autochthonous—in biology, descended from the original flora, fauna or inhabitants of a region; in geology, a rock or mineral deposit that was formed in the area it is found

Autochthony—originating or formed in the place they were found, indigenous

Autochthonic—originating or formed in the place where found, indigenous

Autogenous—produced independent from an external cause or influence

Autognosis—knowledge of oneself, ones nature, abilities and limitations, self-knowledge

Autoscopy—an experience where the individual perceives the surrounding environment from a position outside their body

Avatar—the incarnation of a Hindu deity in human form; somebody who embodies an idea or concept

Ave Maria—also called Hail Mary, this is a Catholic prayer asking for the intercession of the Virgin Mary

Avernian—a gate to the upper level of the Underworld that is relatively easy to open; pertaining to Avernus, a lake in Italy famous for its poisonous vapors, which ancient writers believed killed birds; bird-less

Avidity—great eagerness or enthusiasm for something; greed

Avoirdupois—a system of weights based on a pound of sixteen ounces used in English-speaking countries (cf. troy); figuratively, weight or heaviness

Avuncular—one who acts benevolently, like an affectionate uncle

Awl—a tool with a slim metal shaft and sharp point used for punching holes

Axiology—the study of value and the kinds of things that are valuable; the philosophic study of value

Axone—a threadlike extension of a nerve cell that transmits impulses

Azimuth—the angle measured from north, eastward along the horizon to the point where a vertical circle through an astronomical object intersects the horizon

B

Babuism—a derogatory term for the practices of Hindus who had only slight English education

Babur—the fifteenth and sixteenth Persian conqueror of Central Asia and founder of the Mughal dynasty in the Indian subcontinent

Bacchic—riotous drunkenness

Baccy—British informal name for tobacco

Baden Baden—a spa town in southwest Germany on the edge of the Black Forrest that the rich, royals and celebrities visit

Bade—past of bid, to have offered a certain price for something, especially at an auction

Badinage—banter, playful repartee

Badmash—someone aggressive, violent or evil, a hooligan; a mock reproof, especially when scolding children, as in "what badmash made this mess?"

Baedeker—worldwide travel guide books originated by Karl Baedeker in 1827

Bagatelle—a short piece of classical music, often playful and usually on the piano

Bagger—in financial language, a stock that increases tenfold, a stock bought at $1 and sold at $10 a share is a bagger, a stock bought at $10 and sold at $100 is also a bagger

Bahute—a portable chest with rounded lid covered in leather and garnished with nails used to transport personal luggage

Bailiwick—an area of activity in which somebody has specific responsibility, knowledge or ability

Baize—a course and typically green woolen material resembling felt used for covering billiard and card tables

Balaclava—a close-fitting garment covering the head and neck except for parts of the face typically made of wool

Balalaika—a Russian stringed musical instrument with characteristic triangular wooden, hollow body and three strings

Baldachin—a canopy made of cloth erected over an altar, shrine or throne; a canopy carried above a priest in a religious ceremony

Bale—a bundle of something like paper or hay tightly wrapped and bound with cords or hoops

Baleful—threatening or destructive

Baler—a source of evil or suffering, from archaic bale; to gather and fasten material into bales

Ballot—the total number of votes that have been cast in an election

Balsamic—a very dark, concentrated and intensely flavored vinegar made from grapes

Balsamum—obsolete for balsam, an aromatic oily resinous substance used in medicine flowing from various plants; a balsam-yielding tree like balsam fir

Banal—boringly dull and unoriginal, commonplace, predictable, trite, devoid of freshness or originality, hackneyed, sophomoric

Banausic—not reined or elevated; mundane, dull, boring or tedious

Bandeau—French for "strip," a garment comprising a strip of cloth

Banditti—plural for bandit

Bandolier—a soldier's belt with loops for storing cartridges, worn over the shoulder and across the chest

Bannausos—in Greek, Aristotle refers derogatively to mechanics who are people that work for money such as manual laborers, artisans or merchants, the word drives from making from fire or blacksmiths

Banneret—a knight of high rank who is entitled to lead his own men into battle

Barberry—a thorny bush with orange or red berries often used as a garden hedge plant

Barbette—a gun emplacement for terrestrial fortifications and naval ships; a protective circular armor support for a navy's heavy gun turret

Barbican—a fortified outpost, gateway or outer defense for a city or castle; a tower situated over a gate or bridge used for defense

Barcarolle—a song traditionally sung by Venetian gondoliers

Barded—in cooking, covering meat with fat or bacon to prevent drying; defensive armor for a horse

Bardo—in Tibetan Buddhism an in-between or intermediate state such as death and rebirth

Bark—a small sailing ship with masts fixed breadthways with square sails except for the last mast whose sail runs lengthwise fore and aft; a small boat

Barque—another spelling of bark; cf. Braque

Barricado—a barricade; to barricade

Barrow— a wheelbarrow, luggage trolley

Bashlyk—a pointed cloth hood with long ends for wrapping around the neck used in bad weather

Basileus—a Greek term for monarch, contemporarily called kings or emperors

Basilisk—a legendary reptile whose breath was supposed to be fatal

Basinet—a baby's wicker cradle, usually with a hood

Basse—a low popular court dance in the fifteenth and sixteenth centuries, especially in the Burgundian court

Bated breath—from Shakespeare, to reduce the force and intensity of, to restrain, to wait with subdued breathing due to some emotion or difficulty

Bathos—sentimentality, ludicrous sentiment or commonplace; cf. pathos

Bathyscaphe—a free-diving self-propelled submersible with a crew cabin similar to a bathysphere; cf. bathysphere

Bathysphere—a spherical deep-sea unpowered submersible lowered into the ocean on a cable; cf. bathyscaphe

Batman—a British military officer's personal servant

Battement—a movement in dance where one leg is lifted to the front, side or back and then returns to a supporting leg

Batten—a long flat strip of wood or metal used to hold something in place; to strengthen or fasten something with battens

Batture—a river or seabed elevated to the surface

Bavarian—a beverage made of strong tea sweetened with cane sugar, to which an egg yolk, milk and kirsch are added

Bawd—the madam who runs a brothel

Beadle—an official who is caretaker of a synagogue and oversees services; in the Church of England, a minor parish official who ushers and keeps order

Beard—something that diverts attention or suspicion from another; to oppose or confront somebody confidently or disrespectfully

Beati possidentes—in law, the privilege of the possessor not to have to prove the legality of his passions

Beatific—to be blissfully happy

Beau monde—the world of fashionable society

Beau sabreur—one that carries or fences with a saber; a cavalryman

Beaux—boyfriends or male admirers; men dressed smartly in fashionable clothes

Bed-in—in British engineering, to fit parts together accurately; to make settled and able to work efficiently in harmony

Bedlamite—a madman, lunatic

Beech-mast—the edible nuts of the Beech tree, especially when lying on the ground

Beetling—jutting out and bushy, e.g. beetle brows; to go somewhere quickly

Beeves—plural of beef, in reference to two or more cows prepared for slaughter or carcasses

Begum—a title of respect or high rank for a woman in some Muslim communities

Belfori—same as belfry, the part of a bell tower steeple in which the bells are housed

Belial—a name for the Devil

Belletristic—writing that is valued for its elegance and aesthetic qualities rather than human interest or moral lesson

Belvedere—a building or part of a building positioned to offer a good view

Bema—in a synagogue, a raised platform from which the scriptures are read; the raised area where the alter is located

Bemused—to be puzzled, muddled or preoccupied; cf. nonplussed

Benandanti—an agrarian fertility cult in northern Italy in the sixteenth and seventeenth centuries, the members of which claimed they could leave their bodies and fight witches; demon hunters who evolved into general purpose evil-hunters

Benefice—an ecclesiastical office to which income from an endowment is attached; revenue from church property that provides a living for the clergy; a feudal estate in land

Besetting—harassing or troubling somebody continually

Bêtes noirs—a person or thing that one particularly dislikes or dreads

Betimes—early; in a good time; in a short time, speedily

Bevette—a type of ribbon noodle pasta similar to spaghetti that has a flat section and a slightly convex shape

Bezique—a nineteenth-century French melding and trick-taking card game for two players

Bezoar—a hard mass of material such as fruit or hair found in the intestines of a ruminant animal once thought to be an antidote to poison, a hard mass of material

Bhakfi—in Sanskrit, attachment, participation, fondness for, homage, faith, love devotion, worship or piety

Bibelot—a small decorative ornament or trinket

Bibliothèque bleue—blue library in French, a type of low quality, small format popular literature published in France from the sixteenth to eighteenth centuries printed on blue paper that dealt with local ephemera

Bibulous—to be addicted to drink

Bicêtre—an eighteenth-century mental asylum in Paris for men

Bier—a table on which a casket or corpse is placed; a wooden frame on which a corpse or casket is carried

Bijou—a small, snug, cozy and elegant residence or business; a jewel or trinket

Bilge—the lower part of a boat below the waterline; dirty water that collects in the bottom of a boat; ridiculous talk or ideas

Binnacle—a support or mounting for a ship's compass

Binomial—consisting of or relating to two names or terms; in math, an expression made of two terms linked by a plus or minus sign; in biology, a pair of Latinized words forming a scientific name in the classification of plants, animals and microorganisms

Biotic—relating to life and living organisms or that caused by living organisms; cf. antibiotic

Biretta—a stiff hat worn by Roman Catholic clerics with three upright sections meeting in the center at the top

Birther—a person who holds the view that former U.S. president Barack Obama was born outside the United States and thus ineligible to be president

Bissextile—a leap year, a calendar containing one additional day in order to keep a calendar year synchronized with the astronomical or seasonal year; having an extra day of a leap year (such as February 29th)

Bitterns—a wading bird of the heron family that lives in reeds and marshes; the bitter liquid that is left after salt crystallizes from sea water

Bitumen—a sticky, black and viscous liquid petroleum found in natural deposits or may be refined, also known as asphalt or pitch

Blackguard—a dishonest or unprincipled person

Blancoe—a compound used mostly by British soldiers to clean and color their equipment

Blandishment—enticing action or speech in order to flatter or coax

Blatherskite—somebody who enjoys silly or unimportant chat, a talkative person; chat about silly or unimportant things

Blazon—in heraldry, a coat of arms; to proclaim something widely or ostentatiously

Blini—a small Russian pancake made with yeast and buckwheat flower

Blogosphere—personal websites and blogs, collectively

Bloud—archaic for blood

Bluejacket—an enlisted man in the navy

Boater—a straw hat with a flat brim, crown and hatband

Bobbin—a cylinder wound with thread used for sewing; a narrow cotton cord used for trimming and binding; a reel, coil or pin

Bodhisattva—a Buddhist deity or being who has attained enlightenment but remains in the human world to help others

Bodice—a woman's vest-like undergarment; the part of a woman's dress above the waist (excluding sleeves)

Boffin—a scientific expert, especially in research, usually regarded as unconventional or absentminded

Bohea—a low-quality black Chinese tea

Bole—the trunk of a tree; reddish brown clay used in pigment

Boll—the rounded seed capsule of plants such as cotton or flax

Bona fide—in good faith, sincere and honest, without any intention to deceive; authentic and genuine in nature

Bondsmen—somebody responsible for a legal bond

Bonobo—a chimpanzee with a black face and hair found in the Congo

Boojum—a fictional character created by Lewis Carroll; a particularly dangerous creature or snark

Book—to charge someone with a criminal offense; to engage somebody, especially as a performer

Boreal—a northern temperate region that has cold winters and warm summers

Borzoi—a Russian dog similar to a greyhound

Borzois—a Russian wolfhound

Boschetto—a group of trees that are close together, a grove

Boss—the round raised part that sticks out like a stud at the center of a shield

Boston—a version of whist in which two decks of cards are used and players bid for the right to name bumps

Botcher—to perform poorly through clumsiness or ineptitude; to repair something clumsily; a hodgepodge

Bougie—a thin, flexible surgical instrument for exploring or dilating a passage of the body; short for bourgeoisie which refers to middle-class Europe and the more affluent class in the United States, sometimes used to refer to the upper class

Boulangism—the French doctrines of military reprisals against German popular in the 1880s advanced by General Boulanger

Boulevardier—a fashionable, sophisticated man of the world who treats life with lighthearted cynicism

Bounder—someone who behaves in a dishonorable or immoral way; an ill-bred social-climbing man

Bourgeois—the middle class whose political, economic and social opinions are determined by property and conventional attitudes and respectability, materialistically oriented, propertied, consisting usually of shopkeepers and merchants

Bourses—a taffeta sack that collects long hair at the back of the neck

Boutonniere—a corsage worn on formal occasions; a deformity in the fingers and toes

Bovine—like an ox; figuratively to be dull, stolid, listless or sluggish

Bow land—a knot in which loops remain invisible such as in shoe-laces and ribbons used for decorating

Bow the knee to Baal—to owe allegiance to the King of Kings, Baal, a Phoenician deity who represented the sun; Jezebel, the Phoenician queen of Ahab sought to supplant the worship of Jehovah with the worship of Baal

Bowelled—disembowelment or evisceration of the gastrointestinal tract

Bower—a shady leafy shelter or recess in a garden or woods; a woman's bedroom, especially in medieval times; a picturesque country cottage

Boyar—a Russian Tsar's right-hand man in medieval times

Brace—the symbols { }; another word for suspenders; on a sailing ship, a rope used to control the spar that extends a sail

Branchidae—a line of ancient priests who ruled the temple of Apollo in Didyma (which belonged to Miletus)

Braque—George Braque was a twentieth-century French painter and print maker known for being the founder of Cubism; cf. Barque

Bravo—a hired assassin

Bravura monitor—one who admonishes and corrects wrongdoers

Brazier—a metal container used for burning coal for cooking or to keep people warm; somebody who works on brass articles

Brevet—a temporary promotion of a military officer without an in-crease in pay

Brevette—French meaning to be patient; to certify

Breviary—a Roman Catholic book that contains daily hymns, psalms and prayers

Brickbat—a cutting remark, caustic comment or unkind criticism

Bridewell—a London royal palace built for King Henry VIII that was converted to an orphanage, place of correction for wayward women, prison and poorhouse; generically any jail or prison

Bright's disease—a historical medical classification of kidney diseases, in modern medicine called acute or chronic nephritis

Brindle—a coat covering for some animals that is gray or tawny with darker streaks or spots sometimes described as subtle tiger striping

Brio—lively energy, vigor

Bromide—a platitude, commonplace or hackneyed remark, or trite generalization used as a sedative to soothe someone's nerves

Bruited—a true or false story that is passed around among people

Bruit—to spread or report a rumor widely

Buboe—swelling and inflammation of a lymph node, especially in the armpit or groin

Bubonic—the most common form of plague that affects the lymph nodes causing buboes, or swollen lymph nodes mostly in the armpit or groin; cf. septicemic, pneumonic

Buckler—a small round shield held by a handle or worn on the forearm

Bucolic—relating to the countryside and/or a rustic way of life

Budmash—an irregular native Indian soldier

Bulbul—a grayish or brownish tropical songbird; a songbird frequently mentioned in Persian poetry taken to be a nightingale

Bullae—same as blister; a rounded bony part of the body; the Pope's official seal

Bullet peas—beans and peas, especially chickpeas and cowpeas; the final loan payment on a term loan excluding interest

Bullock—a young bull; a castrated bull; a two-wheeled vehicle pulled by oxen, an ox cart

Bulrushes—a plant with leaves like grass that grows in wet conditions; a marsh plant; a cattail; a papyrus plant

Bumps of Judas—the anxiety and trepidation felt when contemplating betrayal manifest in the form of goose bumps

Burette—a glass tube with measurement markers used to measure a quantity of liquid

Buridan's ass—Buridan's donkey was offered equal amounts of food to eat but could not decide which one, so he starved to death; figuratively, to lose opportunity due to the inability to choose

Burke—to keep something quiet, to prevent information from becoming known; to evade an issue or question; to murder somebody silently without leaving marks or wounds

Burlesque—mocking a serious matter in an imitating way; a ludicrous incongruous imitation of something; a variety show that often includes striptease

Burnoose—a long, loose hooded cloak worn by Arabs

Bursar—an official in charge of funds, a treasurer, especially in a school or monastery

Busbies—a tall fur helmet worn by soldiers such as some British guard regiments

Buskin—ancient Greek tragic drama; a thick-soled laced boot worn by tragic actors in ancient Greece to make them taller; a calf-length laced boot worn in the Middle Ages

Bustard—a large bird with long legs, round body, long neck and short beak found in southern Europe, Asia and Africa

Bustle—a pad or frame worn under the top of a woman's skirt in the nineteenth century

Busto—a bust, statue

Butt—an archery range; a large cask used for holding wine or ale; a unit of liquid measure (126 U. S. gallons)

Butternut—a Confederate soldier in the Civil War

Button—something that resembles a button

Buxom—full-figured, looking healthily plump and attractive with large breasts

C

Ça ira—the emblematic song of the French Revolution that means "It'll be fine"

Cabal—a group of plotters, clique or coterie

Cabala—also spelled Kabbalah, the ancient Jewish tradition of mystical interpretation of the Bible first transmitted orally using esoteric methods

Cabalism—mystical interpretations or esoteric doctrines

Cabalistic—relating to mystical interpretation or esoteric doctrine

Cabbalist—one associated with the mystical interpretation of esoteric doctrine

Cabriolet—a two-wheeled, two-seater horse drawn carriage with a folding roof

Cacciatore—cooked with mushrooms, tomatoes and herbs, e.g. chicken cacciatore

Cache—to hoard, store, accumulate or collect

Cachet—the stamp of approval from authority; things that bring prestige

Cacique—a native chief; a local political boss

Cacomistle—a nocturnal raccoon-like animal with a dark-ringed tail found in North and Central America

Cacophony—strident and discordant noise

Cadastral—an official land register containing information on the value, extent and ownership of land for purposes of taxation

Cadge—to beg by imposing on another's good will

Caesura—a pause or break in speech or conversation; in music, a brief interruption in a musical piece

Caftan—a man's long belted tunic, worn in countries of the Near East; a woman's long loose dress; a loose shirt or top

Caitiff—a coward

Calcine—to heat a solid to high temperature and convert it to a powdery residue

Calefaction—the act of heating or warming

Calfoutis—a tart made of fruit, typically cherries, baked in a sweet batter

Calfoutrées—something sealed

Calgacus's speech—according to Tacitus, a speech by Calgacus leader of the Caledonian Confederation urging his followers to reject bondage and fight to the last against the Romans, in which he asks them to fight for their freedom

Caliban—a complex and sensitive character whose naïvety leads to foolishness

Calico—a coarse cotton cloth with a bright printed pattern

Callow—immature, inexperienced and green behind the ears

Calomel—a mercury compound used as a fungicide, insecticide and formerly as a purgative

Calumet—a long-stemmed ceremonial pipe used by Native American peoples

Calumny—to slander, smear or make malicious statements in order to damage a reputation

Calvary—according to the Bible, the hill outside of ancient Jerusalem where Jesus was crucified; a time of great suffering and anguish

Calypso—in Greek mythology, a nymph who kept Odysseus on her island for seven years; Caribbean dance music with syncopated rhythms

Calyx—the sepals of a flower, typically forming a whorl that encloses the petals; a cuplike cavity or structure

Cama—a hybrid between a camel and a llama

Camarilla—a group of favorites who surround a king or ruler who have no official authority but influence the ruler behind the scenes

Cambric—a thin, spongy looking white linen or cotton fabric

Cambyses—sixth-century BCE king of Persia famous for conquering the Egyptians

Camden—the American Revolutionary war battle with the British in South Carolina in 1780 that pitted General Charles Cornwallis against General Horatio Gates

Cameo—a stone carved to give a raised design in one color against a background of another, especially a pale head against a dark background

Camera obscura—Latin for "dark chamber," a box with a small hole in one side through which light from an external scene passes, striking a surface and creating images, that would lead to the invention of photography, contrasted with painting an optical image

Cameraro—in Spanish a waiter, steward, bellhop or chambermaid

Camisole—a woman's sleeveless undergarment covering the upper torso; a woman's sleeveless top with thin shoulder straps and straight neckline

Campeau—a lively and cheerful person with passionate energy who scatters energy on too many projects, some of which they never finish

Canaille—the common people, the masses

Canard—a hoax or false rumor

Canary—a bright yellow color resembling the plumage of a canary

Canebrake—land planted or overgrown with cane

Cannae—The battle of Cannae of the second Punic War in 216 BCE in southeast Italy in which Carthaginian Hannibal won and taught the Romans that force cannot always win over strategy

Cantabrigian—a student or graduate of Cambridge University, England

Cant— boring talk full of clichés and platitudes; insincere talk, especially talk of high ideals; the jargon of a group generally looked down upon; underworld jargon

Canter—the smooth gait of a horse, slower than a gallop and faster than a trot, a horse's medium pace

Canticle—a hymn or chant forming a regular part of church service

Cantle—the raised back part of a saddle for a horse

Cantonage coffins—linen or papyrus coffins glued together in many thicknesses that encase deceased bodies

Canute—King Canute the Great, king of Denmark, England and Norway, known at the North Sea Empire in 1035 and considered the most effective Anglo-Saxon king in history

Caparison—a decorative covering for a horse, especially a war-horse; elaborate or rich clothing

Caper—a low prickly shrub of the Mediterranean

Capillary—a narrow blood vessel that connects small arteries with small veins; as fine or slender as a hair

Capitularie—a member of an ecclesiastical chapter; a civil or ecclesiastical decree

Capon—a male castrated chicken

Caprichos—a whim or fancy, caprice; a set of eighty prints by Spanish artist Goya in the late 1700s condemning the universal follies and foolishness in Spanish society

Capricious—impulsive, erratic, unpredictable or whimsical

Captious—faultfinding and nitpicking

Capuchin—a member of Franciscan friars in Italy; a hooded cloak formerly worn by women; a long-tailed monkey with a tuft of hair on its head that resembles a monk's cowl

Caput mortuum—the skull; Latin for "dead head" or worthless remains, used in alchemy to denote a pigment; cf. caput vivens

Caput vivens—the brain; cf. caput mortuum

Carabiner—a specialized shackle like a metal spring-loaded loop used to quickly and reversibly connect components, most notably in safety systems

Caravanserai—in some Eastern countries, a large inn with central courtyard used by caravans crossing a desert

Carcase—the dead body of an animal especially of a slaughtered animal after removal of the offal

Cardamom—the aromatic pods and seeds of a tropical plant used as spice and flavoring; a perennial tropical plant with large leaves that bears cardamom

Carder—a machine for combing fibers of cotton before spinning to remove undesirable fibers

Carding—a mechanical process that disentangles, cleans and intermixes fibers to produce a continuous web of silver suitable for processing

Cardovan—a color between burgundy and rose

Careen—to move at high speed swaying, lurching or swerving from side to side; to carelessly move rapidly

Caret—a mark in a text to show where something such as a letter or word should be inserted

Carillon—a set of bells usually hung in a tower played from a keyboard; a tune played on a keyboard connected to a set of bells

Carmagnole—a short jacket worn by working class militant sans-culottes during the French Revolution

Carmelite—a member or an order of mendicant friars founded around 1155 called Our Lady of Mount Carmel

Carmine—a deep purplish red color; a bright red pigment

Carnifex—an executioner, specifically the public executioner in ancient Rome

Carotid—the large artery on each side of the neck that supplies blood to the head

Carrack—a large trading ship common in the Mediterranean in the fourteenth through sixteenth centuries

Carrel—a place where a person can study in private, e.g. a library

Carriage—the way somebody holds their head and body when walking; a part of a machine that holds and moves another part, e.g. the paper holder in a typewriter

Carrière—Eugène Carrière (1849–1906) was a French painter and lithographer

Carroty—describes red hair; a bright reddish orange color

Carthusian—austere and contemplative Roman Catholic monks and nuns in eleventh-century France

Cartouche—a carved tablet or drawing representing a scroll with rolled up ends used ornamentally; a decorative frame panel containing writing forming an artistic feature; a symbol, pictograph

Casbah—in North Africa, a fortress or palace, the older part of a city, often the market area

Casemate—a fortified compartment on an old sailing ship where a cannon was mounted

Cashier—to remove something (including a person) from a position for doing something wrong, to dismiss with disgrace due to a misdemeanor

Cassandra—somebody whose warnings of impending disaster are ignored

Cassava—a large tuber that is poisonous when raw but like a potato when boiled used as a vegetable in many tropical countries; a tropical plant that produces cassava

Cassis—a syrupy alcoholic French drink made from black currants

Cassock—a full-length, usually black robe worn by priests, assistants and choirs

Castellan—the governor or manager of a castle

Castor—a brown oily aromatic secreted from beaver's glands used in medicine, perfumes and bait

Castoreum—an extract made from the dried perineal glands of a beaver

Castrato—a male singer castrated in boyhood so as to retain a soprano or alto voice

Casuistry—the application of general rules and principles to ethics for resolution; subtle, sophisticated and sometimes deceptive reasoning usually in morals to mislead somebody, specious reasoning; cf. sophistry

Catachresis—the abuse of language

Catafalque—a decorated wooden framework that supports a coffin in a funeral

Catalepsy—a state during which muscles become rigid and remain in any position in which they are placed, a state resembling a trance, common in diseases like schizophrenia and epilepsy

Catamount—a mountain lion

Cataplexy—a sudden inhibiting numbness produced by a shock

Catarrh—medically when the nose and throat are blocked with mucus, usually due to a cold; mucus

Catastrophism—in geology, the theory that changes in the Earth's crust during geological history resulted from sudden violent and unusual events; cf. uniformitarianism

Catechise—to instruct in the principles of Christian religion by means of question and answer

Catechism—instruction in the principles of Christianity using set questions and answers; a book that teaches the basic principles of a subject, especially by repetition

Catechist—an instructor in Christianity, a religious instructor; cf. catechumen

Catechumen—somebody who receives instruction in Christianity, a religious pupil; cf. catechist

Catenary—the curve of a length of heavy cable hanging between two points, or something with this shape

Cathexis—the concentration of emotional or psychological energy in one thing or idea

Catholic—with a small "c" to be broad-minded with universal sympathies, the opposite of narrow; with a capital "C" refers to the Roman Catholic Church; cf. parochial

Catnip—a plant of the mint family with grayish leaves with a strong smell that attracts cats

Caudal—relating to a tail; situated toward the hind part of the body

Caul—the membrane surrounding the amniotic fluid that often covers the baby's head when born

Causa sui—Latin for "cause of itself" or something that is generated within itself; in theology, it is the power of God to perform miracles

Causticity—the noun for caustic, able to burn or corrode organic tissue by chemical action; sarcasm in a scathing and bitter way

Cautery—cauterization or the medical procedure of burning a part of the body to remove or close off part of it

Cavalier—a knight or soldier in former times who fought on horseback; a supporter of King Charles I in the English Civil War; showing an arrogant or jaunty disregard or lack of respect for something or somebody

Cavetto—a hollow architectural molding with a curve that is a quarter circle

Caviare—another spelling for caviar

Caviller—one who cavils, one who makes objections with small and unimportant points and trivial and unreasonable objections

Cavil—to quibble, nitpick or be picayune, to find fault in an irritating manner

Cavitary—relating to or having a cavity.

Cedilla—in some languages, a mark placed beneath the letters c and s that signals a change in the pronunciation of the letter such as "ç" in French; cf. acute

Celandine—a tall poppy plant with yellow flowers and bright orange poisonous sap

Cellarage—a fee charged for storing something in a cellar; a cellar or the amount of space in a cellar

Cenotaph—a monument to someone buried elsewhere, especially commemorating those who died in war

Censer—a container in which incense is burned, typically during a religious ceremony

Centaury—a plant of the gentian family used in herbal medicine

Centenary—the hundredth anniversary of a significant event, a centennial

Centripetal—in physics, acting or moving toward the center of an axis, toward the center; in biology, developing from the perimeter inward; in politics, tending to concentrate power in a central authority

Ceres—in Roman mythology, the goddess of agriculture; the largest asteroid orbiting between Mars and Jupiter

Cerulean—a deep blue color, like the sky on a clear day; azure, cobalt, navy, sapphire

Cession—the assignment of property to another entity, in international law it refers to transferring land by treaty

Ceteris paribus—Latin for "with other things the same" or "with all other things being equal"

Chai—a type of Indian tea

Chaise—a light open two-wheeled carriage for one or more people often hooded drawn by one horse

Chalcedony—a translucent or grayish semiprecious quartz stone

Chalk—in the United Kingdom, not by any means, i.e. not by a long chalk

Chamberlain—the manager of a royal or noble household; the treasurer of a municipality; a Roman Catholic priest who attends the pope

Chamorro—indigenous people of the Mariana Islands

Champenois—a minority of people in the Champagne provinces in France

Chancel—that part of a church near the altar reserved for the clergy and choir separated from the nave by steps or a screen, cf. nave

Chancery court—a court of equity, ruling on matters not covered by common laws

Chanticleer—a rooster, especially in fairy tales; a male domestic fowl

Chantry—an endowment to pay for masses for a founder; a chapel or altar endowed for the performance of chantries

Chapbook—a literary booklet sold by traveling peddlers

Chaplet—a decorative circle of beads or flowers worn on the head; a string of beads used by Catholics for counting prayers; in architecture, a small molding resembling a string of beads

Chard—same as a Swiss chard, a variety of beet whose large leaves are cooked and eaten as a vegetable

Charivari—same as shivaree, a noisy serenade for newlyweds involving the loud banging of objects like pans

Charnel—suggestive of death or a tomb; a building or vault in which bones or dead bodies are placed, a tomb

Charon's ferry—in Greek mythology, Charon is the ferryman of Hades who carries souls of the newly deceased across the river Styx to the world of the dead; a coin was usually put in the mouth of the dead person to pay Charon

Charras—the gum resin of the hemp plant

Charwomen—a woman employed to clean

Charybdis—in Greek mythology, a monster in the form of a dangerous whirlpool at the entrance to the cave of the sea monster Scylla

Chasseur—cooked in rich white wine and mushroom sauce

Chasseurs—cavalry

Chasuble—a loose, sometimes sleeveless outer garment worn by a Christian priest

Chatelaine—a woman who is head of a large household; formerly, a woman who owned or controlled a castle or large house; a chain or clasp worn at a woman's waist to hold keys; cf. major-domo

Chaussée—a historic term used to describe early, metaled rural highways

Cheapen—bargain for

Chela—each pair of hinged pincer-like claws terminating the anterior limbs and typically pointed of a crab, lobster or scorpion; cf. chelicera

Chelicera—either of a pair of pincer-like appendages in front of the mouth in arachnids; cf. chela

Chemism—obsolete for chemical attraction, chemical activity or affinity

Chenille—a tufted velvety cord of yard used in trimming furniture and making carpets and clothing

Cherty—a brittle microcrystalline quartz, a type of silica

Cherubim and Seraphim—guardian angels and amazing heavenly beings described in the Bible, Cherubims are guardians of paradise and Seraphims are glowing beings that surround God's throne

Chervil—also called French parsley, an annual herb used to flavor dishes

Cheval de frise—a defensive spiked tree trunk

Chevalier—a chivalrous man; a member of certain orders of knighthood in France such as the Legion of Honor

Chevaux-de-frise

Chevron—a V-shaped symbol often used on military uniforms; a heraldic ornament in the shape of an inverted V

Chez—at somebody's home or business premise, especially a restaurant

Chiaroscuro—the use of light and shade in paintings; the effect of light and shade in paintings

Chicane—an artificial narrowing or turn on an auto-racing course; in cards, a hand without cards of one suit; to employ trickery or chicanery

Chickpea—a yellow seed cooked as a vegetable for consumption

Chicory—a dried, roasted and ground root used in coffee

Chiffon—a light, sheer fabric typically made of silk or nylon; a cake or dessert made of beaten egg whites to give a light taste

Chiffonier—a tall chest of drawers often with a mirror on the top; a low cupboard sometimes with a raised bookshelf on the top

Chignon—a knot or coil of hair on the back of a woman's head

Chilblain—a red itchy swelling on the fingers, toes or ears caused by exposure to cold or dampness

Chillun—Southern African American vernacular for chile or child or children

Chino—a coarse cotton twill fabric, often khaki-colored used in military uniforms and casual pants

Chintz—a glazed cotton fabric often with bright colored patterns, found mostly in South Asia

Chipotle—a pungent smoked red chili used in Mexican cuisine

Chiropodist—in Canada, medicine that is concerned with the care and treatment of the feet

Chirurgical—archaic for of or relating to surgery; obsolete term for surgery

Chivvy—to urge, pester or harass somebody to make them act quickly

Chivy—to tease or annoy with persistent, petty attacks

Chlamy—short for the green alga chlamydomanas that swims with flagella and is often found in stagnant water

Chladni—Ernst Chladni demonstrated how patterns show the geometry of different violin vibrations and produced a formula that predicts these patterns on vibrating circular plates

Choenix—a dry measure of two pints or greater

Choker—a cloth or ribbon fastened around the neck as an ornament; a high, close-fitting collar such as a clerical collar

Chonies—girls' underwear, panties

Chrism—a mixture of oil and balsam used for anointing in baptism in some churches

Chromatic—relating to or produced by color; relating to notes not belonging to the diatonic scale of the key in which a passage is written; cf. diatonic

Chronos—a Hellenistic deity associated with empirical time divided into past, present and future; cf. Aion

Chrysostom—Saint John Chrysostom (347–407) ecumenical patriarch of Constantinople known for his eloquence

Chthonic—in Greek mythology, relating to the underworld

Chunam—a type of plaster used in India made from shell-lime and sand, a kind of quicklime, plaster or mortar

Churl—a bad-mannered person, someone with bad manners

Chyle—a milky fluid consisting of lymph and emulsified fat that forms in the small intestines during digestion

Chymistry—archaic for chemistry

Cicisbeo—a man who loves a married woman

Cidaris—a genus of pencil sea urchins commonly known as the long-spine slate pen sea urchin

Cimmerian—in Greek mythology, people who lived in a land of perpetual darkness; dark and gloomy

Cincinnatus—told by Livy, a fifth-century BCE Roman general who lead Rome through a time of crisis and briefly became dictator but voluntarily refused lifelong dictatorship and returned to his farm; to voluntarily relinquish power and return to citizenship

Cinda—a girl's name, usually an attractive one; an appellation for a pretty young girl

Cipher—a code, secret message or symbols; somebody who is nobody, a nonentity

Ciphering—to put into secret writing, to encode; to do arithmetic

Circassian—denoting a group of mainly Sunni Muslim peoples of the northwestern Caucasus

Circe's cup—in Homer's *Odyssey*, the sorceress Circe offers Odysseus a cup containing a potion with which she seeks to bring him under her spell, something offered to induce compliance

Circumambulation—in religion, the act of moving around a sacred object or idol; to walk around something

Cistern—in medicine, an opening in the brain, Latin for "box"; cf. ventricles

Cithara—an ancient Greek and Roman stringed musical instrument similar to a lyre

Cithern—variant spelling for cittern, a stringed instrument similar to a lute, with a flattened back and wire strings used in the sixteenth and seventeenth centuries in Europe

Citoyen—French for "citizen"

Civet—a slender nocturnal carnivorous mammal with barred and spotted coat native to Africa and Asia; a strong musky perfume from the civet's scent glands; a ring-tailed cat

Clack— a sharp sound or series of sounds

Claque—an audience hired to applaud a performance, a paid audience; a disapproving term for people who follow, praise and uncritically support rich or famous people

Clavichord—a keyboard instrument of the fifteenth to nineteenth centuries that is the precursor of the modern piano where small wedges strike horizontal strings to produce a soft sound

Clavier—a stringed keyboard musical instrument; the keyboard of a musical instrument

Clementia—mildness and clemency

Clerestory—the upper part of the nave and transepts of a church containing a series of windows to admit light to the central part of the building

Cleruchy—in ancient Greece, a Greek colony consisting of Athenian citizens in a dependent country holding land grants awarded by Athens

Clime—a place with a particular type of climate

Clinamen—Latin for to incline, the Latin name Lucretius gave to the unpredictable swerve of atoms

Cloud-rack—a group of moving clouds; water or ice particles visible in the sky, usually white or grey, from which rain or snow falls when the particles congeal

Coadjutor—an assistant or helper; a bishop who assists a diocesan bishop

Cockaigne—in medieval myth a land of plenty, extreme luxury and ease where all physical comforts and pleasures are satisfied

Cockerel—a young male chicken, usually less than one year old, a young domestic rooster

Cockering—someone involved in cockfighting; same as a cocker spaniel

Cocotte—a promiscuous woman or prostitute; a small dish on which food can be cooked and served

Coda—additional text of a literary work that is not necessary to its structure but gives additional information; a postscript, addendum or afterthought; in music, a final section that adds dramatic energy to the work

Codices rescripti—a list of the oldest Latin Palimpsests with occasional observations on their origin

Codpiece—a cover for male genitals; a covering, flap or pouch attached to the front of men's trousers in the fifteenth and sixteenth centuries, from "cod" or scrotum in English

Coefficient—a number that is placed before a letter that represents a variable in algebra, e.g. the "4" in "4x"

Coenesthesia—the general feeling of inhabiting one's body that comes from its organs' stimuli

Coeval—having the same age, duration or date of origin, equal in age or duration

Cog—a piece that projects from the end of a timber beam designed to fit into the opening of another beam to form a joint; to join two timber beams with a cog; a type of ship in medieval times with flat bottoms

Coglione—an obscene term for a blockhead, literally a testicle

Coif—a woman's close-fitting cap, often worn my nuns

Coign—a projecting corner or angle of a wall or building

Coir—a coarse fiber that comes from coconuts used for matting and ropes

Cojones—a man's testicles; courage, guts

Cokade—a knot of colorful ribbons usually worn on a hat

Colander—a strainer used for draining water from food or washing vegetables or fruit

Colic—a sudden attack of abdominal pain, often caused by a spasm, inflammation or obstruction; excessive crying and irritability of infants

Collard—kale, a variety of kale with a crown of smooth, edible leaves

Collate—to compare pieces of information in detail; to admit a member of the clergy to a benefice; cf. benefice

Collation—a light meal such as a cold collation; the reading of religious texts to monks

Collier—a coal miner; a vessel designed to transport coal

Colocynth—a spongy bitter yellow fruit with green freckles

Colophon—the symbol or emblem in a book that represents the publisher's imprint; the details of the title, printer, publisher and date at the end of a book

Colportage—the distribution of publications, books and religious tracts by carriers called colporteurs

Col—the low point in a ridge of mountains often forming a pass between two peaks

Columbiad— a large-caliber, smoothbore, muzzle-loading cannon able to fire heavy projectiles at both high and low trajectories.

Columbus's egg—a trick that is easy once you know how to do it

Comfit—a candy, a sugar-coated fruit or nut

Compass—to understand something fully and completely, more than the average mind can conceive; to achieve or attain something

Compilation—a thing, especially a book or record that is put together by assembling previously separate items

Compline—time at bedtime; cf. Matins, Lauds, Prime, Vespers

Composting—to convert organic matter to compost; to make a compound or composition of several parts

Comtesse—a countess, the wife or widow of an earl or count

Conatus—a natural tendency, impulse or striving, a central theme of Spinoza meaning the inclination of a thing to persist in its own being

Concatenate—to connect separate units into a system, to bring things together

Concatenation—putting together, bundling, to link things together, a state of being interconnected

Concertina—a musical instrument with a folding middle part that is played by pushing both ends together with the hands and pressing buttons; to fold, crush or push together

Conch—a tropical ocean animal with a large spiral shell; the large often colored shell of a conch used as a horn or ornament

Conchyliomania—madness for collecting shells, which was common in the upper classes in the seventeenth and eighteen centuries

Conciliar—relating to a council, especially an ecclesiastical one

Concretism—the theory or practice of concrete poetry whereby the visual arrangement of words takes precedence over the semantic elements involved

Concupiscentia—inordinate desire

Condign—well deserved and appropriate, fitting

Condottieri—a captain who leads a group of hired soldiers, especially during the Italian Renaissance in the Middle Ages

Confinium—to confine, border or limit

Confraternity—a group of people united in a common profession or purpose, often a group of Christians who have joined to perform charitable acts

Confute—to prove a person or assertion to be wrong; cf. dispute

Coniunctio— used in alchemy to refer to chemical combinations

Conjoint—combining all people or things involved

Conjure—to implore somebody to do something; to perform magic tricks for entertainment

Conjuror—an entertainer who performs tricks involving agility and magic; a magician or someone who summons supernatural forces

Connature—not of the same kind

Consanguinity—a relationship by descent from an ancestor and not by marriage, a relationship by blood

Consarn—a mild imprecation meaning to be damned or confounded, translated as "damnit"

Consensus iuris—law by consent

Consistory—in the Roman Catholic Church, an assembly of cardinals convoked by the Pope; the governing body of a congregation; a council of cardinals with or without the Pope

Consociational—relating to a political system formed by the cooperation of different social groups on the basis of shared power

Consol—a government bond in Great Britain from the mid-1700s that pays perpetual interest and has no maturity date

Conspectus—a general survey or overview of something, a synopsis

Contemn—to treat somebody with contempt, to look down on

Continent—lacking self-restraint, especially in sexual matters

Contradictio in adjecto—Latin meaning a contradiction between parts of an argument as opposed to contradiction between two words

Contraindicated—referring to disadvantageous or potentially dangerous maneuvers in therapy that should not be used due to risk

Contralto—the lowest vocal range for women's voices, below alto and soprano; a low speaking voice of a woman

Contrapuntal—polyphonic music with strong differentiated parts; displaying counterpoint

Contratempo—an inopportune or embarrassing occurrence or situation

Contrefosse—in military jargon, a counter-ditch

Contretemps—an unfortunate occurrence, especially when awkward or embarrassing; a quarrel, argument or falling out

Controvert—to argue strongly against something, to dispute

Conurbation—an extended urban area consisting of several towns merging with suburbs or a city

Conventicle—an unlawful or secret religious gathering; a place where a conventicle is held

Cony—another spelling of coney, a rabbit; rabbit fur used for clothing

Cooptation—members adding others to the group to fill vacancies

Coping stone—same as copestone, a flat stone forming part of the coping of a wall; the highest stone in a wall; a finishing touch or crowning achievement; cf. coping

Coping—the top, typically sloping of a brick or stone wall; cf. coping stone

Copperas—a crude ferrous iron sulfate

Coprolite—a fossilized scat

Coprophiliac—one who has an obsessive and sometimes sexual interest in feces and defecation

Copse—same as coppice, an area of densely growing small trees, especially ones that have been cut back to encourage growth; a grove, thicket or wood

Copula—a verb that links a subject with an adjective or noun such as "some dogs are poodles"; anything that links two things

Copulative—a link or joining; a verb that links a subject with its function

Cordate—describes a leaf that is heart shaped

Corded—a fabric with a ribbed surface; having well-developed muscles visible as ridges or ripples

Cordial—a stimulating or medicinal drink

Cordite—a smokeless explosive made of gunpowder and nitroglycerin

Cordon bleu—a cook or cooking of the highest class; meat rolled around cheese and ham coated with breadcrumbs

Cordon—a line of people such as soldiers surrounding an area to control access

Cordova—a Spanish explorer who discovered the Yucatan; the basic monetary unit of Nicaragua

Cordwainer—a shoemaker who makes new shoes from new leather or cordovan leather

Coretto—a sacred religious room decorated with religious art

Cornel—any plant related to dogwood

Cornelian law—a body of ancient Roman reform laws created by the dictator Sulla (81–80 BCE) that expedited the judicial system and established jury trials in criminal cases, which laid the foundation for Roman criminal law

Cornetcy—the office, rank or commission of a cornet officer

Cornet—in music, a three-brass instrument shaped like a compressed trumpet; a woman's headdress of starched cloth worn in the twelfth to fifteenth centuries; a large white headdress worn by some Christian nuns

Cornice—a projecting horizontal molding along the top of a wall or building

Cornpone—relating to country life and its people being simple, unpretentious and homely

Coromandel—same as calamander, a hard black and brown striped wood used in furniture

Corona—a halo, nimbus, aura or circle of light

Corot—Jean-Baptiste-Camille Corot was an eighteenth-century French landscape and portrait painter

Correctiomelle—a magistrate's court

Cortege—a procession, especially a funeral procession; a retinue of servants or attendants

Corvée—in feudal times, a day of unpaid labor required as a serf for a lord; in Revolutionary France, a period of labor required in lieu of taxes

Corvid—a family of birds that contains crows, ravens, jays and magpies

Corvidology—the study of corvids; cf. corvid

Coryphaeus—the leader of the chorus in ancient Greek drama

Costive—slow to act or speak, hesitant; constipated or causing constipation

Cotentin peninsula—also called the Cherbourg Peninsula, this is a peninsula in Normandy that forms the northwest coast France

Coteris paribus—Latin meaning with other conditions remaining the same, all other things being equal or holding other things constant

Coterminous—areas that share a border; two things exactly alike

Cotillion—a formal evening ball or afternoon dance; a complex French dance popular in the eighteenth century

Couchant—in heraldry, used to describe an animal lying down with its head raised

Countenance—to tolerate, accept or give approval to something; the expression of the face, or a face; composure or self-control

Counterfactual—relating to that which has not happened or is not the case, e.g. if kangaroos had no tails they would topple over

Counterpane—a cover for a bed, a bedspread

Countess—the wife of a count or earl; cf. marquise, duchess

Coup d'état—a sudden illegal overthrow or seizure of a government, a putsch; cf. coup de main, coup de gras

Coup de gras—a decisive death blow; a finishing or decisive stroke; cf. coup de main, coup d'état

Coup de main—a sudden, fierce and successful surprise attack against an enemy; cf. coup de gras, coup d'état

Couplet—two lines of verse that form a unit alone or as part of a poem, especially those that rhyme and have the same meter

Courser—a dog that hunts by sight and not scent; a strong, swift horse

Courtag—an instrumental concert with vocal music

Couturier—an establishment or person involved in the clothing fashion industry who makes original garments for private clients

Couverture—a legal doctrine whereby upon marriage a woman's legal rights and obligations are subsumed by her husband

Covenanter—a militant defender of the Scottish Presbyterian church in the seventeenth century; somebody who makes a covenant

Coverlet—a bedspread, cover, quilt or comforter

Cowl—the hood of a monk's cloak; the hood of a chimney that prevents downdrafts

Cowrie—a tropical invertebrate sea animal with a glossy, brightly colored shell

Cowrie shell—a shell of a cowrie, which is smooth, shiny and usually egg shaped with a long, slit-like opening that is tooth shaped; formerly used as money in parts of Africa

Cowslip—a small plant of the primrose family with long-stemmed drooping flagrant flowers native to grassy areas of Europe, Africa and Asia

Cozen—to deceive, cheat or defraud somebody

–Cracy—a suffix as in bureaucracy means rule, government or power

Cravat—a scarf around a man's neck and tied in front that can be worn on formal occasions instead of a bowtie

Credo quia absurdum—Latin for "I believe because it is absurd," Tertullian's defense of religious faith by denying reason

Credo—also called the Apostles' Creed, this is an ancient statement of the doctrines of Christianity

Crenellate—a gap in the top of a castle wall used for shooting

Creole—a person native to a locality; a person, especially a servant

Crêpe—a thin pancake usually rolled; a fine light fabric with a crinkled surface

Creute—a chalk cave

Crinoline—a horsehair and cotton fabric used for stiffening things; a petticoat of crinoline used to expand a skirt; a skirt with wire hoops worn to expand the skirt

Croaker—a person or animal that croaks; another term for a drum

Crocus—a small perennial spring-flowering plant that comes from corn

Croesus—ancient king of Lydia (c. 560–546 BCE) renowned for great wealth and who subjugated the Greek cities in Asia Minor before being overthrown by Cyrus the Great of Persia

Crone—an old woman who is thin and ugly

Crosier—a staff with a hooked end carried by a Christian priest symbolizing their caring for their congregation as shepherds tend flocks

Crowd on sail—many persons gathering together, a throng or swarm, often disorderly and jostling; the common people, the populace

Cruciform—shaped like a cross

Crupper—a strap attached to a saddle that passes under the tail of a horse to prevent it from sliding forward; the hindquarters of a horse

Cruscantism—the Italian effort to purify the Italian language; cf. Purism

Crypto—a person who adheres or belongs secretly to a party, sect or group; secret or hidden

Cucullatus—Latin for hooded, having a hood

Cui bono—Latin for "who stands to gain," e.g. from a crime, indicating that person might have been responsible for it

Cuirass—armor made of metal or leather for the upper body; figuratively, a protective covering

CUL—in texting, short for "see you later"

Cully—one easily tricked or imposed on, a dupe

Culverin—a long-range heavy cannon used between the fifteenth and seventeenth centuries; a medieval musket

Cumbrous—archaic for cumbersome, large and unwieldy

Cunctation—procrastinating, putting off or delaying to a later time; inactivity due to putting something off

Cuppers—a small container, usually with a handle, used to drink from; what a person is destined to receive, suffer or enjoy in life, somebody's lot in life

Curacy—the position or term of office of a curate

Cura—Latin for care or concern; the name of a divine figure who cared and was concerned

Curate—a member of the Christian clergy who assists priests; the administrator of a museum (cf. curator); to organize and choose the items in an exhibition at a museum or gallery

Curator—the administrative head of a museum, gallery or collection; cf. curate

Curd—the solid substance formed when milk coagulates used for cheese; any food with the consistency of milk curd

Cure—in construction, to harden something, especially concrete

Curés—in French a parish priest

Curio—an object collected for its interest or rarity, an unusual artifact, sometimes a trinket

Curiouser—eager to know something or get knowledge; strange, unexpected or hard to explain; intricate or detailed

Curlpaper—a small piece of paper rolled around a lock of hair and twisted to set a curl

Currant—a small juicy fruit from the small deciduous currant bush; a small dried seedless grape

Curriculum vitae—a short account of one's career and qualifications prepared typically by and applicant for a position; a document that describes your education, work experience

Cur—someone regarded as mean, cowardly or unpleasant, a contemptible person; a mixed-breed dog that is ill-natured or in poor condition

Curvet—a leap by a horse in dressage in which its hind legs are raised just before the forelegs hit the ground

Curvilinear—being a curve or having curved parts, curved; moving along a curved path like a ball following a curvilinear trajectory

Cuspidor—the same as a spittoon, a receptacle for spittle

Cycloid—resembling a circle; in psychology, changing states of depression and elation

Cylster—archaic term for enema

Cynocephali—dog-headed; a tribe of dog-headed men native to Africa and India

Cynosure—something that strongly attracts attention by its brilliance

D

Dactyl—a metrical foot of one long syllable followed by two short syllables in classical verse (cf. spondee); a finger or toe

Dactylic—pertaining to dactyls, animals with a finger or toe; in classical verse, a long syllable followed by two short syllables

Dadoes—the lower part of an interior wall decorated in a different manner than the upper part, often with paneling or paint

Daemon—an evil spirit; a source of evil, harm, distress or ruin

Daeva—an ancient animalistic, destructive, demonic creature with a nasty attitude and who cause plagues and disease

Daimonic—to be daemon like or like a mythological being that is part god and part human

Daltonian—color blindness, color deficiency or decreased ability to see color, from John Dalton, an English chemist

Damask—a reversible cotton linen fabric with a pattern woven into it; a grayish-pink color such as a damask rose

Dandle—to move something lightly up and down; to move a baby or child up and down in a playful or affectionate way

Darnel—a grass commonly found growing as a weed in grain fields

Dastard—a dishonorable or despicable person

Daub—to a spread a substance like paint or cream in a crude or hurried way; to apply paint crudely and inexpertly

Davit—a crane-like arm that holds lifeboats over a ship's deck

De trop—superfluous or excessive, not wanted

Deal—softwood lumber like fir or pine wood, especially when cut to a standard size; a plank or board of deal

Decalogue—the Ten Commandments

Decauville—a narrow-gauge railroad with tracks mounted in sections on transverse metal beams

Decius—Roman Emperor from 249 to 251 CE known for strengthening the state, opposing external threats and restoring piety through state religion

Declaim—to speak formally or theatrically; to recite

Declamation—a rhetorical exercise or set speech; forthright or distinct projection of words set to music; cf. recitative

Déclassé—having fallen in social status

Declension—the process of declining or deteriorating; a downward slope

Declivity—a surface such as a piece of land sloping downward; a downward inclination

Decoction—the extraction of an ingredient from a substance by boiling; a concentrated substance that results from decoction

Décolletage—leaving the neck and shoulders uncovered

Décolleté—cut low at the neckline; wearing a garment that is low cut or strapless

Defalcate—to misuse something, especially money or property, that belongs to someone else and is held in trust

Defilade—fortifications or protection against enemy fire; to set up protective fortifications to protect troops

Degrèvement—in French, a reduction; tax relief

Dégringolade—a rapid decline or deterioration in strength, position or condition; a downfall

Deism—the belief in God based on reason rather than revelation, the rational belief in God, involves the view that God set the universe in motion but does not interfere with how it runs, a philosophy influential in the seventeenth and eighteenth centuries; cf. theism

Deist—one with a rational belief in a remote, impersonal God that is like a force rather than a person

Delenda—things to be deleted or removed; cf. servanda

Della Crusca—a circle of late eighteenth-century European sentimental poets whose name was taken from the Italian Accademia della Crusca, which is an organization of scholars founded in 1583 whose purpose was to purify the Italian language

Delphinium—a tall ornamental plant with flower spikes

Delve and span—from a quote from fourteenth-century English priest John Ball, which was "when Adam delved and Eve span, who then is the gentleman" meaning when the first people were digging in the earth (delving) to grow their own food and spinning cloth (span) for their own clothes, where were the people of privilege (the gentlemen) who live a life of leisure by profiting from others' labor (Ball's point is there were no gentleman, we are all equal, no one is higher than another and no one got a free ride)

Démarche—a diplomatic move, maneuver or protest made orally; a statement or protest made on behalf of citizens of a nation to their government

Deme—a township in ancient Greece; a population of closely related inbreeding species

Dementia praecox—premature dementia often beginning in early adulthood characterized by chronic deteriorating psychotic disorder and rapid cognitive disintegration

Demesnes—the possession and use of your own land (as opposed to the ownership of land occupied by tenants); an extended landed estate; the realm of a monarch

Demigod—an important person treated like a god; a minor god in the hierarchy of gods

Demimondaine—a class of women on the fringes of respectable society supported by wealthy lovers, in the nineteenth and early twentieth centuries, women who were financially supported by wealthy men; people of questionable respectability

Demirep—a person of doubtful reputation or respectability

Demiurgic—in Gnostic and Platonic philosophies, the creator and controller of the material world; a very strong and influential force or personality; a magistrate in ancient Greece

Demus—a friend of Paul who deserts him for the present world rather than the religious one hereafter

Denarius—an ancient Roman coin; a generic name for coins

Denaturation—to take or alter natural qualities; to destroy characteristic properties by heat; to make something like alcohol unfit for drinking by adding a toxic or foul-tasting substance

Denisovan—an extinct species of archaic humans of the genus Homo

Denkmittel—German for all our conceptions and means by which we handle facts by thinking them, a framework of assumptions that we use to interpret how the world works, some say we don't directly understand our experiences but filter them through our denkmittel; the cause of the structure and composition of humans

Deontic—relating to the concept of moral obligation

Dephlogistic—oxygen or oxygen gas; cf. philogostic, phlogiston

Deponent—a verb that inflects like a passive verb but is active in meaning; in law, someone who signs an affidavit or testifies under oath

Depravity—moral degeneracy, immorality, corruption, decadence, evil; cf. pravity

Depute—to choose somebody to be your agent; to delegate work, authority or duties to somebody; to act as a deputy for somebody

Dereflection—a psychological technique of directing a person's mind off a certain goal through positive redirection to another goal that emphasizes assets rather than problems at hand

Derogating—to criticize somebody or something severely; to make something seem inferior or less significant, the treatment of someone or something as being of little worth; to deviate from a norm, rule or law, an exemption from or relaxation of the rule of law; to repeal or abolish part of a law, an immunity or exception in the law

Dérogeance—a grievance for persons who did acts unworthy of noble status, the consequences of which could be loss of rank

Dervise—a Dervish or Turkish monk and in modern times an ascetic of a Mohammedan sect that dances energetically whirling and shouting in a trance-like state—a whirling dervish; figuratively one who whirls or engages in frenzied activity

Descant—to talk tediously or at length

De-severant—a phrase from Heidegger in which Dasein is de-severant, it lets any entity be encountered close by as the entity that it is

Desiccative—to remove moisture from something or become free of moisture; to make something uninteresting, to remove vitality from something

Desiderate—to wish to have or see happen; to feel a need for, to miss or desire, to long for

Desuetude—the state of disuse

Detersive—to discourage somebody from taking action or prevent something from happening, especially by making somebody feel afraid or anxious; to refrain from taking action

Detort—archaic for twist, distort or pervert

Deucalion—in Greek mythology, the son of Prometheus (the creator of mankind) and king of Phthia who build an ark in order to survive the deluge

Deuce—something that is bad or unpleasant

Deus absconditus—a hidden or concealed God

Deuterogamist—the second actor in ancient Greek plays; cf. protagonist, tritagonist

Deuteronomy—a book of the Bible that repeats the Ten Commandments

Device—an emblem or motto, especially when used in heraldry

Devoirs—expressions or acts of courtesy or respect

Dewlap—a fold of loose skin hanging from the neck of an animal, especially in cattle

Dhoti—a loincloth worn by Hindu men

Diachronic—the way something develops and evolves over time like language

Diacritic—a mark above or below a printed letter that indicates a change in the way it is pronounced or stressed; cf. acute, cedillas

Diadem—a crown, wreath, tiara

Diakrisis—distinguishing, hence deciding, passing judgment on, the act of judgment

Diapason—a stop on a pipe organ that controls its tone and characteristic sound; a person or instrument's musical range; a tuning fork, a tuning device

Diaphoretic—a sweat-inducing drug

Diarrheic—pertaining to or exhibiting diarrhea or the passage of three or more loose or liquid stools a day

Diastole—the expansion of the heart chambers during which they fill with blood; cf. systole

Diathesis—susceptibility to a disease such as an allergy or gout

Diatonic—involving only notes proper to the prevailing key without chromatic alteration; cf. chromatic

Didymium—a mixture of metallic elements used to produce colored glass

Diecast—formed by pouring molten metal into a reusable mold

Dietetic—relating to what people eat and drink, or diets; food prepared to suit the requirements of a special diet

Diktat—a statement or order that cannot be opposed; a harsh settlement imposed on a defeated opponent or enemy

Dilate—to become wider, larger or more open as in to dilate the eyes; to speak or write at length on a subject

Dilettantism—cultivating an area of interest such as the arts without real commitment or knowledge

Diluvium—relating to the great Flood described in the Bible; cf. antediluvian

Dint—to drive something in forcefully; "by dint of" means using something, or by the force of something

Dio provvederà—God will provide

Diocese—a district under the pastoral care of a bishop of the Christian church

Dioecious—having male and female flowers on different plants of the same species

Diorama—a miniature representation of a scene, often three-dimensional; cf. panorama

Dioscorides—Pedanius Dioscorides was an ancient Greek physician whose work De Materia Medica was the foremost classical source of modern botanical terminology and the leading pharmacological text for sixteen centuries

Dioscuri—in ancient Greek religion, demi-god cult protectors of sailors and patrons of horsemen and races

Diprotodon—a large extinct marsupial that inhabited Australia during the Pleistocene Epoch

Dipsomaniac—somebody with a habitual and uncontrollable craving for alcohol, an alcoholic person

Diremption—a sharp division into two parts, disjunction, separation; the process of separating something forcefully or violently, to separate or take apart

Dirge—a funeral song, elegy or requiem; a sad or mournful song

Discoid—shaped like a disc

Discomfiture—frustrating feelings of embarrassment or awkwardness

Disconcert—to disturb the composure of, to unsettle

Discordia concors—harmonious disharmony

Discursive—digressing from subject to subject; in philosophy, argument or reasoning rather than intuition

Discussant—a participant in a formal discussion or seminar

Dishabille—a state in which somebody is partially undressed or dressed very casually or incompletely, a state of casual dress

Dismay—to be discouraged or disappointed; to fill someone with alarm, apprehension or distress

Dismission—to refuse to give consideration to something; to consider somebody unsuitable for a particular reason

Disport—to behave in a playful manner; a form of lively entertainment or diversion

Dispute—a disagreement, argument or debate; to argue about something, to discuss heatedly; to compete for, to strive to win; cf. confute

Disquisition—a long formal essay or discussion on a subject

Dissertate—to discusses a subject fully and learnedly, to discourse

Distaff—of or concerning women; a stick or spindle onto which wool or flax is wound for spinning

Distemper—paint mixed with water and a glue-like substance instead of oil used in painting walls, scenery and posters

Distich—two lines of poetry that sometimes rhyme that form a complete unit in themselves

Distrain—same as distress, mental suffering; hardship; the seizure of property for money owed, especially rent

Dithyrambic—passionately emotional speech or writing; in ancient Greece, a wild and impassioned choral hymn

Dittany—an aromatic pink-flowered plant related to oregano cultivated for its ornamental and medicinal properties

Diurnal—happening every day, daily; happening during the day as opposed to at night; in botany, flowers that open during the day and close at night; cf. nocturnal

Divan—a sofa without a back, and sometimes without arms; in former times a smoking room

Divaricate—to branch or fork at a wide angle

Diver—same as diverse, varied

Divers—more than one and of various types, several or many

Divertissement—in ballet, a dance highlighting the dancer's skill rather than the story

Dives—a name for a rich man

Divinum—canonical hours often referred to as the Breviary, is the official set of prayers that marks and sanctifies the time and day of prayer

Doff—to take off or tilt a hat or take a coat or piece of clothing off; cf. donn

Dolce vita—a life of luxury and idle self-indulgence

Dolerite—a volcanic rock similar to basalt containing crystals; same as diabase, an igneous rock of fine- to medium-sized grain

Dollop—a shapeless mass or blob of something; to casually add a shapeless mass or blob to something

Dolorous—involving or causing sorrow or sadness

Donjon—a fortified tower in a medieval castle

Données—a basic fact or assumption on which something else is developed; a theme or subject, especially in a literary or theatrical work

Donnish—resembling, characteristic of or stereotypical of a university professor; one displaying erudition or being absent minded

Don—to put on a garment (cf. doff); the Spanish equivalent of mister or a Spanish gentlemen or aristocrat; the leader of a Mafia crime family; a university college teacher, especially at Oxford or Cambridge in England

Dormice—a nocturnal rodent of the family Gliridae found in Europe, Africa and Asia accustomed to long periods of hibernation

Double entendre—a remark that is ambiguous and sexually suggestive

Dovecote—a structure with many openings used for housing pigeons

Doxic—Greek word for common belief or opinion, to appear, to seem; beliefs based on opinion

Doxie—another spelling for doxy, a set of beliefs, especially religious beliefs

Drab—lacking brightness or interest; drearily dull; cf. dribs and drabs

Dragoman—an interpreter or guide, especially in countries speaking Arabic, Turkish or Persian

Dratted—used for emphasis, especially to express annoyance or irritation

Draught—United Kingdom spelling of draft; the round flat piece used in the game of checkers; spelling for draft, drafty, a slight wind

Dressage—the training of a horse to carry out a series of precise controlled movements in response to minimal signals from its rider; cf. goormay

Dressur—a chest of drawers; a sideboard with shelves above for storing and displaying plates and kitchen utensils

Drib—a small amount; cf. dribs and drabs

Dribs and drabs—in small scattered or sporadic amounts; cf. drib, drab

Drill—a tough thick cotton fabric twill like khaki used in work clothes and uniform; a shallow furrow in which seeds are grown

Dromedary—a type of camel with one hump on its back

Dropsy—an old term for the swelling of soft tissues due to the accumulation of excess water, same as edema, the buildup of excess fluid between tissue cells

Dross—something worthless or of low quality; the scum formed on metal usually from oxidation

Drover—a broad-edged stone chisel used for dressing stone; a person who moves groups of animals such as cattle or sheep

Dry guillotine—in France, prisoners' slang for being sent to Devil's Island in French Guiana

Dryad—in Greek mythology, a nymph inhabiting a forest or a tree, especially an oak tree

Ducal—relating to a duke or dukedom

Duchess—the wife of a duke; a noblewoman of the highest hereditary title of nobility; cf. countess, marquise

Ducility—capable of being hammered out, thin, as in certain metals; malleable

Ductile—malleable enough to be worked like metal that can be hammered into shapes; able to be molded or shaped; easily persuaded or influenced

Duenna—a woman governess to a younger woman, especially in former Spain

Dulce nec decorum est pro patria mori—Latin for "it is sweet and honorable to die for one's country" written by the Roman poet Horace

Dun—a brownish grey color, as in a dun complexion; darkly bleak and depressing

Dunciad—The Dunciad is a satire by Alexander Pope celebrating dullness and its agents that bring decay, imbecility and tastelessness

Dunkel—describes several dark German lager beers, dunkel in German means dark

Duodecimo—a book size created by folding paper to give twenty-four pages

Durance—to imprison or confine

Durbar—an official reception held by a prince or British governor in colonial India

Durry—a type of Indian rug; to roll paper and tobacco into a durry

Durst—archaic past tense of dare

Dyad—two individual units linked as a pair; in music, a chord consisting of two notes

Dyspepsia—indigestion; figuratively to be in a bad mood

Dysthymia—chronic mild depression

E

Ebriety—the condition of being drunk; the state of being thrilled or exhilarated

Ebriosity—the state of being regularly drunk; the feeling, thrill or excitement of being intoxicated from alcohol, especially if habitual

Ecce Homos—a portrayal of Jesus Christ crowned with thorns

Ecchymotic—a discoloration due to extravasation of blood, as in a bruise; cf. extravasation

Ecclesia pressa—in the Classical Age, the era of heathen persecution of Christians and subsequent Christian martyrdom

Ecclesia—the Latin term for the Christian Church; the principle assembly of ancient Athens during its Golden Age

Ecclesiology—the study of the history and theology of the Christian church

Eccyclema—in classical Greek theater, a low platform stage mechanism that rolled on wheels and revolved on an axis that could be pushed on stage

Echelon—the level of authority or rank in organization; the lower echelons of society; in the military, a formation where units are positioned behind and to one side of those in the front in a stepped manner so each has a clear view ahead

Eclat—great brilliance, as in performance or achievement; conspicuous success; great admiration or applause; ostentatious display

Eclogue—a pastoral poem, usually in the form of a dialogue between two shepherds

Écossaise—a Scottish country dance popular in France and Britain in the late eighteenth and early nineteenth centuries

Ectomorphic—a person who is tall and thin with long lean limbs; cf. endomorphic, mesomorphic

Ectypal—a reproduction or copy; cf. archetypal

Ecu—an ancient French coin

Ecumenical—encouraging different Christian churches to work and worship together; cf. oecumenical

Educable—capable of being educated or taught

Educe—to elicit or derive something; to develop something or make apparent

Effendis—in Asia and North Africa an important or well-educated man; in Turkish the equivalent of "Sir"

Eidetic—able to recall or reproduce things previously seen with startling accuracy, clarity and vividness

Eidos—the distinctive expression of the cognitive or intellectual character of a culture or social group

Ejusdem farinae—Latin for "death calls made that night"; of the same flour, figuratively "from the same stable"

Ekstasis—from ancient Greek, to be or stand outside oneself, a removal to elsewhere; the state of being beside oneself or rapt out of oneself

Elastic—capable of returning to its original shape after being deformed, compressed or expanded as in an elastic waistband; cf. elatic

Elatic—same as elastic, capable of stretching; in economics sensitive to changes in price

Elecampane—a plant with a tart and bitter flavor

Electrum—a pale-colored alloy of silver and gold used in jewelry and ornaments

Elenchus—an argument that refutes a proposition by proving the opposite of its conclusion, a logical refutation, especially one that disproves a proposition by proving the direct contrary of its conclusion, commonly used by Socrates in the Socratic dialogue

Eleusinian mysteries—in ancient Greece, the cult of Demeter held secret religious rites recalling the abduction of Persephone from her mother Demeter by Hades while holding beliefs such as an afterlife; cf. Eleusis

Eleusis—in ancient Greece, the place where the cult of goddess Demeter existed and the religious Eleusinian mysteries occurred; cf. Eleusinian mysteries

Elicit—to call forth, draw out or provoke

Elide—to nullify or annul; to ignore; to cut off or omit in pronunciation, such as a vowel, usually the final one

Ellipsis—in speech or writing a word that is superfluous or able to be understood contextually

Ell—something L-shaped or with a right-angled bend; an obsolete English measurement of forty-five inches used to measure cloth

Elysian fields—an evolving Greek concept of the afterlife from Homer with a beautiful meadow where we experience perfect happiness, Virgil where the dead are judged worthy and the Aeneid with poetry, singing and dancing

Embay—to enclose as in a bay, to surround or envelop

Embonpoint—roundness of body shape caused by excess weight, plumpness; a woman's breasts or chest

Embouchure—the position and use of the lips, tongue and teeth in playing a wind instrument

Embower—to shelter something in a bower or structure resembling a bower

Embrasure—a small opening in a parapet of a fortified building, splayed on the inside

Embrocate—to rub lotion or liniment onto a part of the body

Embrocation—a lotion or liniment that relieves muscle or joint pain

Emetic—that which causes vomiting

Emeute—from French, an uprising, rebellion or riot

Émigré—an expatriate, emigrant or exile

Eminent—of superior position, fame or achievement; high or in a raised position; cf. immanency, imminent

Emmer—wheat cultivated in ancient times used for fodder

Emmet—same as ant

Emoji—a digital image used to express an idea or emotion

Emolument—a payment for work done

Emphyteusis—in Roman and civil law, a contract by which a landed estate leases to a tenant either in perpetuity or for a long term of years

Emphyteutic—a long-term lease in civil law, a long-term lease of land or buildings, sometimes in perpetuity

Empiric—somebody who exclusively relies on observation and experiment to determine truth rather than theory; a charlatan or quack, especially in medicine

Empyrean—the sky, heavens or celestial sphere; in Greek and Roman times, the highest part of heaven containing pure fire or light and thought to be the dwelling place of God

Empyreumatic—having the odor of burnt organic matter as a result of decomposition or heat

Emulous—seeking to match or rival another's achievement; motivated by rivalry or imitation; to emulate

En bloc—all together or all at the same time

En clair—in diplomatic jargon a message sent in ordinary language and not in code or cipher

En passant—in passing rather than the full focus of someone's attention

Enceinte—pregnant; a defensive wall or enclosure; a place protected by a wall or enclosure

Enclitic—a word that depends on a preceding word for its formation or pronunciation

Encomiastic—a speaker or writer of an encomium, someone who gives high praise

Encomiast—somebody like a speaker or writer who gives high praise; someone who gives an encomium

Encomia—to praise someone or something highly

Encyclopaedist—a writer or editor of the sixteenth-century French reference work *Encyclopédie*, which was a reference work that advanced secular, technical and political ideas of the period

Encyclopedists—one who writes for an encyclopedia; one of the writers of the French encyclopedia (1751–1780) who were identified with the enlightenment and advocated deism and scientific rationalism

Endive—a plant with tightly packed curly leaves used in salads

Endogamy—the custom of marrying a member of one's social group; cf. exogamy, polyandry, polygamy, monogamy

Endogenous—having an internal cause or origin; not attributable to any external cause; confined within a group or society; cf. exogenous

Endomorph— stocky build with a prominent abdomen; cf. ecotomorph, mesomorph

Endomorphic—a person who is stocky with a prominent abdomen; cf. ectomorphic, mesomorphic

Endue—to endow somebody or something with an ability or quality

Endymion—in Greek mythology Endymion was a handsome shepherd prince, Zeus offered him his choice of destinies and he chose immortality and youth

Enervate—to weaken or lessen the vitality of a person; cf. attenuate

Enfeoff—to invest somebody with freehold land

Engadine—a long, high alpine valley region in the eastern Swiss Alps

Engrail—to indent something with small curves, to ornament the edge with curved indentations, to mark the edge of a coin with small curved notches

Engram—a hypothetical physical impression made in neural tissue by a mental stimulus once regarded as the source of memory

Engranger—French meaning to bring in or rake in such as profits

Enology—the study of wine and the making of wine

Enounce—to pronounce a word clearly and definitely; to state something formally or officially

Enragés—French meaning to be furious or in a rage

Ens creatum—Latin meaning being created

Ens rationis—a thing that has only rational or mental being, an abstract entity with no positive existence outside the mind

Ens—an actual entity, as distinct from a quality or characteristic, an existing thing

Ensete—a genus of flowering plants and genera of the banana family native to regions of Africa and Asia

Entablature—in classical architecture, the section of a structure that lies between the columns and the roof, it comprises the architrave, frieze and cornice

Entail—control of the dead over the living; in law, to restrict the future ownership of real estate to particular descendants through instructions written into a will

Entailment—in law, the process in which a property cannot be sold or devised by will so the property passes to an heir (it is intended to keep property in the main line of succession)

Entelechy—the real and not theoretical existence of a thing; the life force believed to be responsible for the development of living things

Enteritis—inflammation of the intestine, commonly the small intestine

Enterologist—a practitioner of the branch of medicine concerned with disorders of the digestive system and intestinal tract

Entheogen—a psychoactive substance used in religious contexts to attain a mystical experience, generating the god within

Enthymematic—an argument in which the premises or conclusion is unexpressed or incomplete that often contains implied premises

Enthymeme—an argument that assumes premises with their obvious elements omitted thus forming an illogical sequence

Entrechat—in ballet, a leap in which the dancer's legs are crossed rapidly in the air and the heels are beaten together

Entrement—Old French for between servings, a small cuisine or dish served between courses or simply a dessert

Entresol—a low story between the first and second floor of a building; a mezzanine Comminatory—threatening, punitive or vengeful

Enucleate—to remove the nucleus from a cell; in surgery, to remove intact from its surrounding capsule

Eo ipso—Latin for by that itself, by that fact alone

Epact-the difference in days between a solar year and a lunar year

Eolithic—relating to the earliest period of the Stone Age during which stone tools began to be used

Epée—a sharp pointed dueling sword designed for thrusting; the sport of fencing with an epée

Ephebic—in ancient Greece, a young man who has just reached manhood or full citizenship undergoing military training

Ephemeride—an insect of the mayfly family that emerges in summer from a larval stage under water that lives only hours as an adult

Epicanthic fold—the fold of skin from the eyelid that partially covers the part of the eye nearest the nose common in Asians

Epicene—having both male and female characteristics; neither male or female; lacking vigor and strength, weak; a male who has female characteristics

Epicharis—Roman noblewoman who conspired against Emperor Nero and was caught and tortured but bravely never revealed her co-conspirators

Epidemiology—the study of epidemic diseases and their control

Epigastric—the upper middle region of the abdomen

Epigone—a mediocre imitator of somebody else, especially an important actor or philosopher

Epigram—a concise, witty and often paradoxical remark or saying, a witty form of expression; a short poem expressing an idea in a satirical and witty way

Epilegomena—a backward-looking analysis intended to understand past circumstances on which to build in order to clarify problems and issues; a second phenomenon associated with and apparently due to another

Epileptoid—a thing resembling epilepsy or with sudden spasms

Epiphyte—a plant that grows on another plant but does not depend on it for nutrition, such as moss

Epirrhema—in ancient Greek comedy, an address usually about public affairs spoken by the leader of part of the chorus after they had sung an ode; cf. antiepirrhema

Epithalamium—a poem or song written to celebrate a wedding

Epoché—an ancient Greek word meaning to suspend judgment, later used by Edmund Husserl to bracket an idea in order to suspend questionable judgments in order to accurately understand phenomena

Epode—in classical Greek drama the part of a lyric ode that follows the strophe and antistrophe; cf. strophe, antistrophe

Eponymous—having the name that is the name of something else

Equerry—an officer in a royal household responsible for horses; in the British monarchy, a personal attendant to the monarch or member of the royal family

Equine—relating to horses

Ere— earlier in time, before

Erewhile—a while ago, a time ago

Ergot—a cereal disease caused by a parasitic fungus; dried ergot fungus containing psychologically active substances used in medicine to treat migraines or initiate labor in pregnancy

Erinyes—same as the Furies, in Greek mythology, three terrifying snake-haired, winged goddesses (Alecto, Megaera and Tisiphone) who punished wrongdoing, sometimes considered the handmaids of justice

Erinys—the daughter of Thanatos, the god of death, who served as his messenger

Erlebnis—in German, an insight that comes suddenly, such as understanding how to solve a difficult problem

Ermine—a small northern weasel

Eros—the Greek god of love; sexual love or desire; cf. Thanatos

Erotomaniac—excessive and insatiable sexual desire; the delusion of being romantically involved with another person, especially someone famous

Errare humanum est—Latin meaning to err is human but to persist in error (due to pride) is diabolical, sometimes attributed to Seneca the Younger

Erysichthon—the Thessalian king who chopped down the sacred grove of the goddess Demeter in order to build himself a feast hall, as punishment the goddess inflicted him with insatiable hunger that drove him to exhaust his wealth, become impoverished and finally devour his own flesh; metaphorically, one who is destroyed by their own desires

Erysimum—a flowering plant popular in gardens, wallflowers

Erysipelas—a severe skin rash accompanied by fever and vomiting caused by streptococcal bacterium

Escalade—an attack involving the use of ladders to scale the walls of a fortification; to climb a wall with ladders

Eschatological—a body of religious doctrines concerning the human soul in relation to death, judgment, heaven and hell

Escheat—the reversion of property to the state (or in feudal law a lord) on the owner's dying without legal heirs

Escorial—a vast building complex in central Spain near Madrid containing a monastery, palace, church and mausoleum built for the Spanish sovereigns

Escutcheon—a shield or emblem bearing a coat of arms; ornamental metal around a keyhole, door handle or switch

Esoteric—intended for or understood by only a few; difficult to understand; secret or highly confidential knowledge; cf. exoteric

Espagnolisme—a passionate temperament; cf. logique

Espèces—French for cash

Esperanto—an artificial language devised in 1887 as an international language based on some principal European languages

Espontoon—a sort of wooden pike or shaft six feet long with a metal blade

Esquire—a courtesy title placed after a man's full name, especially the name of an attorney; showing one is an attorney; an unofficial title of respect

Esse—sum, to be; cf. potesse

Ester—an organic often fragrant compound formed between acid and alcohol without water

Ethnography—a branch of anthropology dealing with the study and description of ethnic groups

Etiological—causing or contributing to the development of a disease; serving to explain something from a cause or reason for it, often in historical or mythical terms

Etiology—the philosophical investigation of causes and origins; in medicine, the investigation into the causes and origins of diseases; the set of factors that contribute to the occurrence of a disease

Euboia—a large fertile Greek island northeast of Attika

Eucharist—the symbolic bread and wine eaten and drunk during the ceremony of Communion

Euchre—a card game where each player receives five cards and must take at least three tricks to win

Euergetism—from Greek meaning "doing good deeds," which was an ancient practice of wealthy individuals who distributed part of their wealth to the community, also called evergetism

Eugenic—selective breeding in order to improve humans

Eulogium—praise bestowed on a person or thing, a panegyric or eulogy

Eumenides—in Greek mythology, three sister goddesses identified with the Furies, avenging goddesses

Eunomia—a condition of good order, as in a society or state

Euphonium—a brass instrument similar to a small tuba used in military and brass bands

Euphuistic—a literary style in the sixteenth and seventeenth centuries with excessive use of alliteration, antithesis and simile; an affected literary style; pompous language

Evanescent—disappearing after only a short time and soon forgotten, fleeting

Evince—to show a feeling or quality clearly, to show clearly; to indicate something by action or implication, to reveal

Evitable—capable of being avoided, avoidable; cf. inevitable

Ewer—a large jug with a wide mouth used to carry water to wash in

Ex cathedra—Latin for "from the cathedral" or "from the throne" originally designating decisions made by Popes from their thrones; with the authority of status or rank, with authority

Ex hypothesi—Latin meaning according to the assumptions made, by hypothesis, in accordance with the hypothesis

Excelsior—a word used to name hotels, newspapers and other products to indicate superior quality

Excogitate—to think out, plan or devise

Excrescence—a growth that sticks out from a body; an ugly, unsightly addition or extension from something like a building

Excreta—any waste matter discharged from the body such as feces and urine

Excursive—digressing from the main topic usually in a rambling and wordy way

Excursus—a lengthy digression from a main topic

Execrable—extremely bad or of very low quality; detestable, worthy of being excreted

Exemplum—a brief story used to illustrate a moral point or an argument

Exogamy—the custom of marrying outside one's social group; cf. endogamy, polyandry, polygamy, monogamy

Exogenous—relating to or developing from external factors; cf. endogenous

Exophthalmia—protruding eyeballs

Exordium—the beginning or introductory part, especially of a discourse or treatise

Exoteric—capable of being understood my most people and not just an informed sect; understandable; cf. esoteric

Expiatory—to make amends, show remorse, suffer punishment for wrongdoing or atone for wrongdoing

Expiry—coming to an end or no longer valid after a period of time, ending or ceasing; death, especially death of a person

Extension—indicates the meaning of the set of objects in the world to which the word corresponds, e.g. human nature means the various characteristics of what constitutes human nature; cf. intension

Extramundane—outside or beyond the physical world

Extravasation—to leak or cause blood or other fluid to leak from a vessel into surrounding tissue as a result of injury, burns or inflammation

Extraversion—same as extroversion, a personality type interested and involved in people and things outside themselves

Extreme unction—a sacrament in which a priest prays for the recovery and salvation of a critically ill or injured person

Exudate—any substance like sweat exuded from cells or organs, to exude substance

Ex-voto—a religious offering given to fulfill a vow

Eyrie—another spelling of aerie, the nest of a bird of prey, usually in a high, inaccessible place; a building, especially a stronghold in a high, inaccessible place

F

Fabulist—a writer of fables; a teller of fanciful stories, a liar

Facture—the manner in which something like a painting is made

Faggot—another spelling of fagot or a bundle of sticks to be burned as fuel; a bundle of pieces of metal used for welding

Fainéant—unwilling to do anything, idle; a lazy person

Fain—to be pleased or willing under the circumstances; with pleasure, gladly

Fakirs—a religious Muslim who lives by begging; a Hindu ascetic who lives by begging and endures extraordinary feats of physical endurance

Falange—a Fascist movement founded in Spain in 1933 and the only legal party in Spain under the regime of Franco

Fallibilism—the philosophic principle that human beings could be wrong about their beliefs or understanding of the world yet still justified in holding incorrect beliefs

Falsetto—a method of voice production used by male singers, especially tenors, to sing higher notes than their normal range

Fanfaronade—empty boasting, bluster

Fanominon—an observable fact or occurrence or a kind of observable fact or occurrence

Fantod—nervous anxiety, nervousness

Farinaceous—containing or consisting of starch

Faro—a seventeenth-century French gambling card game

Farthingale—a hooped petticoat or circular pad of fabric around the hips formerly worn under women's skirts to extend and shape them

Fascine—a large bundle of brushwood; a long piece of wood used to line or fill a trench

Fatback—fatty meat from pork usually dried and cured by salt

Faun—in Roman mythology, a rural god with the body of a man and legs and horns of a goat regarded as the source of strange voices

Faux-bourdon—in the fifteenth century, a music technique employing three voices with the upper and lower voices progressing and the middle voice extemporizing

Fédérés—an annual celebration during France's revolutionary era, derives from the Fête de la Federation

Fedet—a mounted sentry or scout

Fellaheen—in an Arab country, the laboring class that lives off the land

Fellah—in an Arab country, a member of the laboring class who lives off the land

Felucca—a small sailboat with triangular sails used in the Mediterranean Sea

Fen—a low-lying marshy land often drained and cultivated due to its nutrient-rich soil

Ferruginous—containing or resembling iron; a reddish brown color, like rust, rust-colored

Ferule—a flat ruler with a widened end, formerly used to punish children

Fetlock—a part of the lower leg of a horse between the knee and hoof

Fetor—a strong foul smell as in the fetor of decay

Fez—a red flat-topped hat with a black tassel on top worn by men in some Muslim countries, formerly the Turkish national headdress

Fichu—a woman's triangular lightweight scarf worn around the neck in the eighteenth and early nineteenth centuries

Fictive—creating or created by imagination

Fideism—the view that religious knowledge depends on faith and revelation

Fidejussor—archiac for one who gives security

Fie—expressing disapproval, annoyance or disgust with somebody or something

Fife—a small high-pitched flute often used in marching bands

Figura—a figure; a statue

Filariasis—a tropical disease caused by a microscopic worm spread by flies

Filiation—in law, the judicial determination of the paternity of a child, especially one born out of wedlock

Filibeg—the kilt or pleated skirt worn by Scottish Highlanders

Filibuster—in the military, a mercenary or irregular in a revolutionary army of a foreign country, a military adventurer abroad

Filigreed—delicate, decorative openwork made from thin twisted metal; a delicate ornamental tracery

Fillet—a fleshy boneless piece of meat near the loins or ribs of an animal; a band or ribbon worn around the head, especially for binding the hair; to remove the bones from something like a fish; in architecture a raised or sunken ornamental surface between larger surfaces; a plain or decorated line impressed on the cover of a book

Fillip—something that acts as a stimulus or boost to activity

Fin de siècle—relating to or characteristic of the end of a century, especially the nineteenth century

Finial—a distinctive ornament at the apex of a roof pinnacle or canopy

Firkin—a small cask formerly used for liquids, butter or fish; a unit of liquid volume equal to about eleven gallons

Firmament—the sky, considered as dome; a field or sphere of an interest or activity; a selection of premium clothing

Fisc—treasury, a public treasury, from Latin fiscus or a money basket

Flacon—a small, often decorated bottle with a tight fitting cap

Flagon—a container for beverages with a handle, narrow spout and sometimes a lid

Flail—to strike or hit something

Flambeau—a lighted torch made of wicks dipped in wax; a large decorative candlestick

Flâneur—an idler or loafer

Flatus vocis—in philosophy, the nominalist's description of the use of names that do not correspond to objective reality

Flaxen—a pale grayish yellow color of flax; made from flax fibers; fair-haired, fair, blond, golden-haired

Fléche—a slender spire, especially on a church; a military field-work consisting of two faces framing a salient angle with a gorge

Flense—to strip the skin or blubber from a whale or seal

Fleshpot—a place that provides sexual entertainment and gratification

Fleur-de-lys—a king of France heraldic with three petals tied with a band

Fleur-de-lis—a stylized iris that is used as a decorative design common in French heraldry

Flie—the space above a stage where scenery and lighting can hang out of the audience's view

Flint—a very hard grayish fine-grained form of quartz that produces sparks when struck with steel used in prehistoric times to make tools

Flinty—to be hard, inflexible, stern and unemotional

Floruit—flourished, abbreviated as "fl" before the name of a past person indicating their era

Flute—a rounded groove running down an architectural column

Fluviatile—pertaining to or peculiar to rivers; found near rivers

Foemen—an enemy in war; a foe

Foie gras—the liver of a specially fattened goose or duck prepared as food

Foison—archaic for a plentiful crop or good harvest; to have plenty; vitality, strength and ability

Folie à deux—French for "a madness shared by two," a shared psychosis where delusional beliefs are transmitted from one individual to another

Folk-mote—a folk meeting, general assembly of the people of a shire or town

Fomentation—instigating or stirring up undesirable sentiment or actions; archaic for poultice (cf. poultice)

Fontanel—a soft, membrane-covered space on a young baby's skull

Foolscap—a cap worn by jesters; a conical cap for slow or lazy students; a standardized size of paper in Great Britain, usually thirteen by sixteen inches

Fop—a man who is concerned with his clothes and appearance in an affected and excessive way, a dandy

Foppery—a foolish man overly concerned with his appearance in seventeenth-century England

Foppish—a man obsessed with fashion who is so vain about his appearance it becomes ridiculous

Forborne—the past participle of forebear, to have held back from acting or to have been patient when annoyed or troubled

Foregather—to assemble or gather together

Forfend— to defend, secure or protect, to ward off, protect or preserve, to fend off or avert; archaic, to forbid

Forma mentis—a noun, a type of word whose meaning determines reality (nouns provide the names for all things, people, objects, sensations, etc.)

Forse—maybe, perhaps, possibly, may or might

Forsooth—archaic for indeed, in truth

Fosse—a wide trench usually filled with water for defense, a trench

Foundling—an abandoned baby with unknown parentage

Frait—rotten, from Latin meaning soft and mellow

Franciade—in the French Republican calendar, the period of four years at the end of which it was necessary to add a day to the calendar to keep it aligned with the solar year; an unfinished epic poem by Pierre de Ronsard

Francs-tirearus—the former unit of currency in France, Belgium and Luxembourg

Francs-tireurs—French for "free shooters" or irregular military formations deployed by the French during the Franco-Prussian war, also known as guerrilla fighters

Frangible—fragile or brittle

Frangipani—a deciduous tree with perfumed flowers native to tropical America; a perfume derived from frangipani flowers

Frappé—a frozen fruit-flavored desert; in ballet, the hitting of the foot on the floor

Freebooting—to plunder or loot

Fricassee—a dish of stewed or fried pieces of meat served in a thick white sauce

Frieze—a wall painting, a band of decoration running along the wall of a room, usually just below the ceiling; in classical architecture, the horizontal band forming part of the entablature of a classical building, situated between the architrave and cornice and often decorated with sculptured figures

Frigorific—the vaporization of liquids is frigorific or a cooling process, causing coldness

Friuli—a region in the northeast corner of Italy boarding Austria and Slovenia

Friulian—relating or characteristic of the historic European region of Friuli or its inhabitants; cf. Friuli

Frog—an offensive term for a French person; a decorative fastening for the front of a garment consisting of a loop of braid or cord and a button that fits into the loop

Froings—a word-working tool with one blade fastened at right angles to a short handle used to split wood along its grain to make shingles or barrel staves

Frond—a large leaf divided into many thin sections, especially in ferns and palms

Frontlet—a decorative band worn on the forehead; an animal's forehead, especially a bird's when colored differently; the decorative border on the front alter in a Christian Church

Fructidore—the twelfth month of the French Republican calendar

Frugivorous—an animal that eats mainly fruit, fruit-eating

Fuddle—to make a person confused, especially with alcohol; to drink too much alcohol regularly

Fug—a stale or airless atmosphere, a stuffy atmosphere

Fugleman—somebody acting as a leader and example for others, a leader; a solider used to teach drill movements by performing them

Fugue—a musical form that first states a theme, which is repeated and varied with accompanying contrapuntal lines; a disordered state of mind in which someone wanders from home and experiences a memory loss relating only to the previous environment

Fulgurate—to flash like lightning; in medicine, to destroy unwanted tissue with electricity

Fulguration—to flash like lightening, a flash; in medicine, to destroy unwanted tissue with high-frequency electricity

Fuller—a half-round hammer used for grooving and spreading iron; a tool for reducing the area of a piece of work; a groove running along the flat of a sword blade

Fulling—a dress made with lots of fabric and not close fitting

Fulminant—exploding violently; an illness coming suddenly with severe symptoms and short duration

Furbelow—a gathered strip or pleated border of a skirt; to adorn with trimmings

Furniture—equipment and accessories used for activity; metaphorically, accessories or abilities needed to accomplish something

Furuncle—a boil on the skin, a skin inflammation

Furze—same as gorse, a spiny bush with yellow flowers and black pods

Fusilier—a solider armed with a lightweight musket

Fusty—fetid, moldy, damp, stale; stuffy, old-fashioned, antiquated, dull, boring

Futurity—the future as a concept; an event that has not happened yet but will in the future

G

Gadarene—rushing headlong without thinking, moving fast without thinking

Gage—something given as security until a debt is paid or obligation fulfilled; a token or object that is thrown down as a challenge to fight; to challenge to fight

Galatia—an ancient land located in central Turkey

Gall—a feeling of bitterness or resentment; something that angers or irritates; the feeling of annoyance or anger; a sore on the skin of an animal caused by friction; to cause a sore on the skin by rubbing; a swelling on a plant caused by insects, fungi, bacteria or damage; the contents of the gallbladder, bile; a metaphor for bitterness

Gallicism—a word or phrase of French origin used in another language; characteristic of the French

Gape—to stare with the mouth open, to look at somebody in surprise or wonder with an open mouth; to open the mouth wide; to open or split apart with a gap

Garret—a room at the top of a house immediately below the roof, an attic

Gasconade—bravado, boasting, blustering, to boast extravagantly

Gathers—that part of a garment that is gathered or drawn in

Gauche—lacking grace or tact in social situations

Gaucherie—a lack of grace or tact in social situations, social awkwardness; a socially awkward act

Gaud—a showy trinket or ornament, a gaudy bauble

Gauleitier—a district leader in Nazi Germany who served as a provincial governor; a subordinate political official resembling a Nazi gauleitier; a local tyrannical official

Gaure—a large wild ox with a dark coat native to southeastern Asia

Gawpe—to stare with the mouth open in wonder or astonishment; to gape

Gazette—a local newspaper; an official publication with governmental news

Gefilte—stuffed fish, a dish made from a poached mixture of ground deboned fish

Gemmule—a reproductive structure produced by asexual reproduction in sponges, a reproductive bud

Generatio aequivoca—spontaneous generation

Gen—in the United Kingdom, same as information

Genius loci—the character, atmosphere or spirit of a place

Genus irritable vatum—meaning the irritable race of poets, from Horace

Geognosy—the study of the origin and distribution of minerals and rocks in the Earth's crust

Gerund—a noun formed from a verb describing an action, state or process using an –ing in English, e.g. "smoking" in "no smoking"

Gerundive—a Latin adjective ending in "–ndus" formed from a verb and meaning "that must or ought to be done"

Gesta dei—meaning hearing is almost as good as seeing, from Dei gesta per Francos by Guibert, who believed relating read history was as good as observed history

Gestalt—a set of things such as a person's thoughts or society's mores considered as a whole in such a way that they amount to more than the sum of the parts

Gethsemane—the garden outside Jerusalem where Jesus went through agony and arrest; a place or occasion of great mental or spiritual suffering

Gewgaw—a showy inexpensive object, a trinket

Ghassanide—an early Arab tribe situated on the western side of the Syrian Desert

Gibbet—a vertical post with a horizontal beam from which executed criminals' bodies were hung for public display; to execute by hanging; to display a body after execution; to expose somebody to ridicule or contempt, especially in publication

Gig—a light two-wheeled carriage pulled by horses; a light, fast narrow boat adapted for rowing or sailing; a small light rowboat carried on board a sailing ship

Gigante—Spanish for giant

Giggle—to laugh in a silly, high pitched way (laughter based on intensity ranges from chuckle, titter, giggle, chortle, cackle, belly laugh and the sputtering burst)

Gill—a unit of measure in the United Kingdom equal to a quarter of a pint in the United States

Gills—the vertical plats on the underside of mushrooms; the wattles or dewlap of a foul

Gimcrack—showy or superficially appealing but badly made and worthless

Gimlet—a tool for boring holes in wood consisting of a slim metal rod with a sharp corkscrew end

Gingé—an often pejorative nickname for a person with red hair

Gingham—a light plain-weave cotton fabric with checks in white and another color, e.g. a gingham dress

Glacis—a long gentle slope, especially in front of a fortification; neutral ground between opposing forces

Glissando—sliding a finger or thumb up or down a keyboard or harp strings to create a smooth change in pitch between two notes; a sliding movement on a violin or trombone to change pitch from one note to another

Gloam—archaic for twilight, dusk, a back-formation from gloaming

Glossist—a time traveler; a writer of glosses or comments; one who tries to conceal

Gneiss—a coarse-grained rock formed at high pressures and temperatures with visible light and dark bands

Gnocchi—an Italian dish made of dumplings from potatoes and flour and usually served with a sauce

Gnomic—containing proverbs or pithy sayings that express some basic truth; matters that are opaque or difficult to understand

Gnomology—an ancient Greek word for "charming garden ornament" but also "thought" or "judgment" which changed over time to refer to sentences containing thoughts, judgments or aphorisms; a collection of gnomes or maxims and adages

Gnomon—the arm of a sundial that shows the time of day by the position of its shadow

Gnosis—possessing knowledge, especially spiritual truth such as claimed by the early Christians

Gnosticism—a pre- and post-Christian philosophy/religious movement characterized by the doctrine that emancipation comes through knowledge, the possession of which saves initiates from the clutches of matter; cf. gnostic, gnosis, agnostic, agnosticism

Gnostic—pertaining to knowledge; an adherent of Gnosticism; cf. gnosis, Gnosticism, agnostic, agnosticism

Goad—a stimulus, something that encourages an activity or process to begin

Gobbet—a quantity of liquid, often in a sticky blotch; an extract from a text, especially chosen for comment in an examination

Godown—a warehouse, especially in Asia

Goiter—enlargement of the thyroid gland appearing as swelling in the front of the neck often due to iodine deficiency

Golconda—a rich mine; broadly, source of great wealth, from Golconda, India known for its diamonds

Golgotha—same as Calvary, a site outside Jerusalem where Jesus was crucified, the biblical name for the place Jesus was crucified

Goormay—the senior member of a group; a form of competitive horse training; broadly, the taming of any kind of animal; cf. dressage

Gorget—a nun's headdress that covers the neck and shoulders; a crescent-shaped piece of armor that protects a soldier's throat; a crescent-shaped necklace

Gorge—the neck of a bastion or other outwork; the rear entrance to a fortification

Gott—German for god

Gourd—a hard-skinned fleshy fruit related to cucumbers and squash, often used for decoration or hollowed as cups

Graecize—to imitate the Greeks, to Hellenize

Graffito—an ancient drawing or inscription on a wall or rock

Graphomania—also known as scribomania, is the obsessive impulse to write

Greave—a piece of armor worn from the ankle to the knee, shin armor

Grenadier—a British soldier belonging to the Royal Household's Guards Division; a soldier with exceptional height and ability

Griffin—a mythical monster with the head and wings of an eagle and body and tail of a lion

Grip—a suitcase

Grippe—an archaic term for influenza

Grisaille—a method of painting in gray monochrome, typically to imitate sculpture

Grisette—a young, working-class French woman

Groat—crushed grain, usually oats

Groin—a sea wall built out into a river or the sea to prevent land erosion; the area between the tops of the thighs and the abdomen; the genitals, especially the testicles

Grosso modo—roughly, circa or approximately

Grossvater—a seventeenth-century German traditional folk dance tune

Groundling—a spectator or person of inferior taste, such as a member of a theater audience who traditionally stood in the pit below the stage

Groundnote—the key note, basic or prevailing tone; cf. headnote, heart note

Gryllos—a fantastical creature that is part human and part animal

Guadgrind—a character from Dickens's book *Hard Times* who pursues profitable enterprises, his name is used to refer to someone who is only coldly concerned with facts and numbers

Guava—a pear-shaped tropical fruit with red or yellow skin and pink flesh; a tropical tree that produces guavas

Guerdon—a reward or recompense

Guidon—a pennant that narrows to a point or fork commonly used as a standard for a light cavalry regiment

Guignol—a character in a puppet show who represents the silk workers in France

Guildenstern—a character (along with Rosencrantz) from Shakespeare's *Hamlet* who embodies a brown-noser, a sycophant

Gule—a large octagonal motif used in patterns on Oriental rugs that resembles a rose with straight-sided petals

Guondam—that once was, former

Gutta-percha—a hard, tough thermoplastic substance that is the coagulated latex of certain Malaysian trees used in dentistry and electrical insulation

Gymnosophist—ancient ascetics of India who went naked and practiced meditation and mystical contemplation

Gyre—a circle or spiral; a circular or spiral motion or form; in literary use, a whirl or gyrale

Gyve—a fetter or shackle

H

Haarlem—a historic city in the Netherlands on the Spaarne River near Amsterdam

Habiliment—clothing; special clothing associated with somebody's work, position or occasion; equipment and gear needed for a task or activity

Habitello—a religious penitential garment

Hack—a taxi; a horse for riding or driving

Haft—the handle of a knife, ax or other weapon or tool, a handle

Hagiography—a biography of a saint; a biography that treats its subject with undue reverence

Halberd—a combination ax and pike used in medieval times

Halliard—another spelling of halyard, a rope used to raise or lower something like the sail

Halt—to have flaws or inconsistencies in poetic rhythm

Hamadryad—in Greek and Roman mythology, a minor deity who lives in a tree and dies when the tree dies

Hamann—German philosopher Johann Georg Hamann who opposed the scientific Age of Enlightenment because scientific reason only leads to doubt or denial of the reality of the world; he emphasized aesthetic experience

Hammam—a Turkish bath similar to a steam bath or sauna

Hamper—equipment on a ship that is essential but likely to get in the way; a large basket with a cover for laundry or food

Handsell—promotion of books by personal recommendation rather than publisher-sponsored marketing

Hap—in Scotland, a cover for a person or a bed such as a cloak or comforter

Happed—fortune, chance, one's luck or lot

Haras—a horse breeding establishment, a horse stud farm

Hard-smiting—to hit hard like hard-smiting swords

Harem—a generic term for domestic spaces reserved for women in a Muslim family

Haring—to run with great speed

Harlequin—a comic actor usually shown wearing multicolored diamond patterned tights and a black mask

Harpy—in ancient mythology, a female monster in the form of a bird with a human face; in classical mythology, a wind spirit creature; the neotropical harpy eagle also known as the American harpy eagle; an offensive term for a bad-tempered nagging woman; a predatory person

Harrow—a farm machine with sharp discs used to break up soil; to break up land by pulling a harrow over it, to till or plow

Hauberk—a knight's long, often sleeveless tunic made of chain mail

Hausfrau—a traditional housewife considered to be mostly interested in her home and family

Hauteur—haughtiness of manner, disdainful pride

Hawser—a heavy cable that is used when mooring or towing a ship

Hayti—the name for African Americans who settled in North Carolina after the Civil War; the community came to be known as Hayti, which whites commonly used for black settlements; the former name of the island Republic of Haiti

Headnote—a brief summary, comment or explanation that precedes something; cf. groundnote, heart note

Headstall—same as headpiece or head decoration; in printing, an ornamental design printed at the beginning of the text; the part of the bridle that goes around the horse's head

Heart note—in perfumery, the core element of fragrance that gives a perfume its distinctive character; cf. headnote, groundnote

Hebephrenic—schizophrenia characterized by disorganized speech and inappropriate behavior

Hebetude—mental dullness or lethargy

Hecatomb—in ancient Greece and Rome, a public sacrifice and feast; a large-scale sacrifice

Hector—to bully, intimidate, harass, hassle, badger

Heeltap—a small portion of liquor remaining as in a glass after drinking

Hegira—the withdraw of Muhammad from Mecca to escape persecution; in Muslim dating, the first day Muhammad withdrew from Mecca, which is 622 CE in the Georgian calendar

Heliocentric—with the sun at the center; measured from the center of the sun

Heliometer—a telescope that is used to measure small angular distances between astronomical objects

Heliotrope—a bluish purple color; a hairy plant of the borage family; a cultivated plant of heliotrope flowers that are purple and fragrant

Hellebore—an early flowering often poisonous perennial plant of the buttercup family with large divided leaves native to North America, Europe and Asia

Hellespont—the narrow strait in northwestern Turkey connecting the Aegean Sea and Sea of Marmara, now called The Dardanelles

Helpmeet—a helpmate, a companion and helper; a husband or wife

Heme—a deep red portion of hemoglobin that contains iron

Hemistich—in Old English, a half of a line of verse

Hennaed—a red dye made from plant leaves; a rich reddish brown color

Herbalize—characteristic, consisting or made of aromatic herbs

Herboriste—a noun, a word whose meaning determines reality such as things, people, objects, feelings, etc.

Heresiarch—a leader or founder of a heretical religious group or movement

Heriot—in feudal England, a tribute or gift given by a tenant or villein's family to his lord upon the tenant's death

Herm—a square stone pillar with a carved head on top, typically of Hermes, used in ancient Greece as a boundary marker or signpost; a bust on a pillar

Hermagoras—an ancient Greek rhetorician and teacher of rhetoric in Rome

Hermeneutics—the science of interpreting texts, especially the Bible; in theology, explaining or interpreting religious concepts, theories and principles

Hermetica—Egyptian-Greek wisdom texts from the second century CE presented as dialogues in which a teacher, usually called Hermes Trismegistus, enlightens a disciple

Hermione—in Greek mythology, the daughter of Menelaus and Helen

Hesperian—relating to the West, from Greek meaning of the evening; in mythology, Hera's orchard called the Garden of Hesperides in which an apple tree produced golden apples that grant immortality when eaten

Hetaerae—a courtesan or mistress, especially one in ancient Greece

Heteronomy—living subject to others' laws or laws imposed by other people or institutions; when parts of an organism have different modes of development, growth and function

Hexis—a Greek word meaning a relatively stable arrangement or disposition such as in health or character

Hidalgo—a member of the Spanish or Portuguese nobility, the feminine term is hidalga; a Spanish nobleman of the lowest rank

Hiding—a beating, trouncing or thrashing

Hieratic—relating to priests; in linguistics, relating to the stylized traditional ancient Egyptian arts; an ancient version of Egyptian hieroglyphics

Hierophant—somebody who interprets and explains obscure and mysterious matters, especially sacred doctrines or mysteries; in ancient Greece, a priest who revealed mysteries

Hierosgamos—sacred or spiritual marriage

Hillock—a small hill or mound

Hilt—the handle of a sword consisting of a guard, grip and pommel

Himation—an ancient Greek loose outer garment consisting of a large cloth draped over one shoulder and under the opposite arm

Hinc et nunc—here and now

Hippocras—a medieval spiced wine sweetened with honey

Historie événementielle—history seen as long-term historical structures; cf. Historié mentalité

Historié mentalité—history seen as the history of attitudes; cf. Historié événementielle

Hitching—to move in an awkward jerky way; obstacles in the way of progress

Hither—to or toward this place; situated on this side

Ho—an offensive term for a prostitute or women in general

Hobble-skirt—an Edwardian era narrow, nearly skin-tight skirt that forced women to take tiny geisha-like steps

Hock—the joint in the hind leg of four-legged animals such as a horse corresponding to the human ankle; a cut of cured meat taken from the lower joint of the leg immediately above the foot

Hod—a V-shaped tray on the end of a long pole usually carried on the shoulder used to carry bricks, mortar and other building materials; a coal shuttle

Hodful—a quantity that may be carried at one time in a hod, such as a hodful of coal

Hodman—same as a hod carrier, somebody who carries bricks and mortar in a hod

Hodology—the study of pathways as in neuroscience and the interconnection of brain cells

Hollandaise—a rich sauce made of butter, egg yolks and lemon juice

Holovere—in the Middle Ages, the name of an imperial dye

Homaloidal— relating to straight lines and planes; satisfying the axioms of Euclidean geometry; flat in the form of a plane

Homeopathic—a disease treatment system where a patient is given minute doses of a substance that in larger doses would produce symptoms of the disease

Homeopathy—the treatment of disease by minute doses of natural substances that in a healthy person would produce symptoms of the disease; cf. allopathic

Homeostasis—an inner equilibrium

Homiletical—relating to a homily; relating to the art of writing and preaching sermons

Homing—a dwelling place together; capable of returning home, usually over long distances

Hominy—food made from corn kernels that are soaked in an alkali solution of either lime or lye

Homo faber—the human being as the maker or creator

Homoeomeria—the state of being homogeneous in elements, likeness or identity of parts

Homoerotica—the tendency to obtain sexual gratification from a member of the same sex; homosexual activity

Homoiousianism—a Christian who believes Jesus Christ is similar to but not God; cf.

Honnête home—a well-educated, non-pedantic man of manners at home in both the salon and his study

Hoopoe—a bird with a prominent crest and downward curving beak and loud cry native to Europe, Asia and Africa

Hopple—same as hobble, to fetter the feet of an animal

Horology—the art of making watches and clocks

Hors concours—that which is not competing for a prize; something unrivaled or unequaled

Hors de combat—literally "outside the fight"; a French diplomatic term referring to combatants who are incapable of waging war such as sick or wounded enemy prisoners

Horsed—a Scottish term for a lengthy, rampant session of charged sexual intercourse often fueled by alcohol

Hortensius—ancient Roman orator and politician and opponent of Cicero in the Verres trial; a book by Cicero whose theme is that genuine happiness comes by embracing philosophy

Hospitaler—a member of a European crusader military order in the eleventh century; a member of a religious charitable order involved in caring for the sick

Houris—in Islam, a beautiful young woman who attended Muslim men in paradise; an attractive woman

Housatonic—a river that originates in western Massachusetts, flows south through Connecticut and empties into Long Island Sound

Housewife—a sewing or mending kit

Hove—the nautical past tense of heave, e.g. to have hoved a line

Howdah—a large seat for several people sometimes with a canopy on the back of an elephant

Huetius—Pierre Huet (Huetius in Latin) was a seventeenth-century French churchman and scholar who founded the Academie du Physique in Caen

Huissier—an usher

Humanitas—Latin for human nature, civilization and kindness

Humectant—a substance that absorbs or helps retain moisture such as a skin lotion

Hummer—low, continuous, indistinct noises; a droning sound

Hummock—a small hill or mound; a ridge of ice in an ice field

Hurdy-gurdy—a mechanical musical instrument played by turning a handle, such as a barrel organ; a medieval string instrument played by turning a crank that causes strings to vibrate while being controlled by a keyboard

Hustings—political activities such as speech-making and organizing public rallies that take place before an election

Hutment—a group of huts forming a military encampment

Hydromel—a drink similar to mead made with fermented honey and water

Hydroptic—pertaining to hydropsy, dropsical, thirsty

Hyletic—relating to matter, material or solids having physical form

Hyperion—the moon of Saturn; in Greek mythology, one of the Titans, son of Gaia and Uranus

Hyperplasia—increasing the number of cells; cf. hypertrophy

Hyperthymic—to have mild manic traits

Hypertrophy—increasing the cell size; cf. hyperplasia

Hypocritical—falsely claiming high principles, hypocritical

Hypostasize—to assume the reality of, to attribute a real reality, such as an idea or proposition; to assume a fundamental reality; something that settles at the bottom of a fluid

Hypostatic—the essence or reality of something; in Christian doctrine one of the three parts of the Trinity; in Christianity, the essential nature of Jesus in which the divine and human are combined

Hypostatize—to treat something conceptual as if it were real, to give an idea concrete existence

Hypostyle—a classical building with a roof or ceiling that rests on many columns

Hypotheses non fingo—Latin for "I feign no hypothesis" or "I contrive no hypotheses" made famous by Sir Isaac Newton meaning ideas do not necessarily need to be correct in order to be good

I

Iamb—a metrical foot of one short or unstressed syllable followed by one long or stressed syllable; cf. imbic

Iambic—a poem written in iambs; cf. iamb

Iatrogenic—relating to illness caused by medical examination or treatment

Ibise—a tropical wading bird with a downward-curving beak

Ibsenite—a follower of Norwegian playwright Henrik Ibsen who is known for his realism in such plays as Peer Gynt where he examined the realities behind social facades, criticized contemporary morality and examined the real conditions of life

Icarus—in Greek mythology, the son of Daedalus who drowned in the sea while attempting to escape from Crete after the sun melted his wings of wax

Icosahedron—a three-dimensional geometric figure with twenty sides, a twenty-sided figure

Ideation—to form an idea of something, or form ideas

Idées recues—a French phrase for a received or accepted idea such as a generally held opinion or concept

Ides—in the Roman calendar, the fifteenth day of March, May, July and October, and the thirteenth day of the other months

Idiopathic—describes a disease or disorder that has no known cause

Igneous—rock formed under conditions of intense heat produced by the solidification of volcanic magma; relating to or characteristic of fire

Ignoratio elenchi—known as the irrelevant fallacy, a fallacy in logic where a point is supposed to be proved or disproved by something that is not an issue

Iliac—relating to the ilium and its surroundings; cf. ilium

Ilium—the wide flat upper portion of the pelvis that is connected to the base of the vertebral column

Illicit—illegal, unlawful, illegitimate, criminal, against the law; cf. licit

Imago—in psychology, an unconscious idealized mental picture formed in childhood, especially of a parent

Imbrication—in architecture, the overlapping of tiles or slates; overlapping like roof tiles; to overlap or be overlapped

Imitatio Christi—the attempt to live and act as Christ lived and acted

Imite—also imitar, imitation or imitative, to imitate or follow as a model

Immanence—existing within or inherent in something; describing a God that exists in all parts of the universe

Immanent—existing within or inherent in something; describing God as existing in all parts of the universe; cf. eminent, imminent

Imminent—about to happen or threatening to happen; cf. immanence, eminent

Immure—to confine someone in prison; to enclose something in a wall or surround something with walls

Impasto—a technique in art of applying paint thickly so that the strokes can be seen; paint thickly applied

Impecunious—having little or no money, unable to live a comfortable life, poor; cf. pecunious

Imperforate—lacking an opening, not perforate

Impertinent—brash, showing bold or rude lack of respect; not appropriate or relevant, irrelevant; cf. pertinacity

Impetigo—a contagious bacterial skin infection that causes pustules and yellow crusty sores

Implacable—impossible to pacify or reduce in strength, not to be appeased or mollified; cf. placable

Importune—to harass persistently to do something

Impost—a customs duty; a weight a horse must carry in order to be handicapped in a race; the top part of an often decorated pillar capped with a vault or arch

Impostume—an abscess

Imposture—the act of pretending to be somebody else in order to trick people, deception

Imprimis—Latin for in the first case; an introduction to a list of items or considerations

In actu—Latin for actually

In anima—the inner self of an individual, the soul

In camera—in private, secret; in closed court where the public is barred; in the judge's private chambers

In folio—a large sheet of paper folded once in the middle making two leaves or four pages of a book or manuscript; a book or manuscript of the largest common size consisting of folio folded sheets

In partibus infidelium—in the territory of unbelievers or in the regions of infidels, abbreviated in partibus or i.p.i.

In partibus—a bishop whose title is from some old see who has fallen away from the Catholic faith

In posse—a large group with a common purpose

In rebus—representation of a word or phrase in pictures or symbols often presented as a puzzle

In rem—Latin for "in the thing itself"; a lawsuit against property and not a person; cf. ante rem

In vivo—existing inside a living organism

Inadvertence—done unintentionally or without thinking, resulting from carelessness; failing to pay attention or take enough care; cf. advertence

Inanition—exhaustion caused by lack of food or water or as a result of disease; lethargy or lack of vitality

Incarnadine—a crimson or blood-red color

Incipient—beginning to appear or develop, initial, embryonic, budding

Incipit vita nova—Latin for to enter a new life, or thus begins a new life

Incredulous odi—unable to believe, to dislike

Incubus—something that causes much worry or anxiety such as a nightmare or obsession; in medieval times, a male demon that was believed to have sex with women while they were asleep

Incunabula—the early stages or beginnings of something

Indigo—a deep purplish blue color; blue dye

Indissociably—unable to be separated, disconnected or considered separately, inseparably linked

Indissolubly—incapable of being undone, broken or dissolved

Indite—to write or compose something such as a letter or speech

Indole—a crystalline compound used in perfumes

Inerrant—incapable of making a mistake; containing no mistakes

Inevitable—unavoidable, certain, predestined, fated: cf. evitable

Inextricable—impossible to get free from; impossible to disentangle or undo; extremely complex

Infatuate—to make somebody act irrationally as a result of temporary passion

Infibulation—to close the vagina of a woman by stitching with the clitoris often removed, common in some African cultures

Infimum—in mathematics, the greatest element of the containing set that is smaller than or equal to all elements of the subset

Ingle's accident—ingle is anatomically the groin, figuratively it is thus the pejorative product of the groin such as a catamite, paramour, favorite or sweetheart; to coax, cajole or wheedle

Ingle—a fireplace, an open fire burning fireplace

Inimica—Latin for unfriendly, hostile, harmful, also inimicus

Inimitable—impossible to imitate, especially due to being a unique person or group, unique

Inlaid—laid up or away in a place of concealment

Innet—an astrological acronym for life path, eight individuals who are full of energy and confidence and have an extraordinary ability to focus

Innominate—without a name, nameless

Inquietude—physical or mental restlessness or disturbance

Insensate—unable to feel or sense; lacking sense or understanding, lacking common sense, foolish; lacking in sympathetic feeling or human kindness

Insipid—dull, bland, characterless, colorless, flavorless; cf. sipid

Instaure—to renew or renovate; to instaurate

Insurgent—a rebel against authority, especially one who belongs to a rebellious group

Intaglio—a carving made by cutting from a hollowed out design in material such as stone; in printing, an engraving where the design is cut into the plate instead of protruding from it

Integument—an outer protective layer; the protective cover of an animal such as a shell or skin

Intendant—an administrative official, especially in former France, Spain and Portugal

Intenerate—to make tender

Intension—indicates the meaning of a word or name that assumes the word has an intrinsic and is thus analytic, e.g. there is an essence in human nature; cf. extension

Inter alia—Latin for among other things, when one wants to say there is more involved than what they are mentioning

Inter se—Latin for among or between themselves

Intercalation—to insert an extra day or month into a calendar in order to keep it consistent with the solar year; to place something into something else or inserting it between other parts

Interdict—a court order that prohibits something; a ban imposed by the Roman Catholic Church excluding a person or nation from the Church

Interferometer—an instrument in which two beams of light are used to make precise measurements

Interlard—to vary or interrupt speech or writing by interspersing contrasting material, to insert something different

Interlineate—to insert words between lines of writing in a text or document

Intermezzo—a short connecting instrumental movement in a musical work; a short piece of music for a solo instrument; a light dramatic, musical or other performance inserted between acts of a play

Intermit—to discontinue doing something temporarily, to discontinue temporarily; to pause for a short time

Interpenetrate—to penetrate thoroughly, permeate

Interposition—to say something that interrupts what another is saying; to place yourself between two people or things; to intervene or interfere in a situation

Interstice—a small opening, crack or gap; a small space in a tissue or between parts of the body

Intestine—relating to the internal affairs of a state, as in an intestine war; internal

Intimate—to imply or hint

Intone—to say something in a slow, serious and solemn way; to sing the opening phrase of the Gregorian chant; to speak with a rise or fall in the pitch of the voice.

Intra muros—Latin for "within the walls"

Intramural—situated or done within the walls of a building; taking place within a single educational institution; situated or done within a community

Intranaut—an individual who explores or reflects on their own mind in search of meaning; cf. astronaut

Intransitive—a verb without a direct object, e.g. the verb "die" in "he slowly died"; with no direct object

Intromission—the insertion of something into something else, an insertion

Intumesce—to become enlarged or swollen due to increased blood, to swell with blood or other fluids

Inveteracy—being obstinate or persistent; tenacity

Inveterate—firmly established and of long standing; fixed in habit or practice, especially bad ones

Invidious—making or implying an unfair distinction; unpleasant because it could produce jealousy, resentment or hatred

Invita Minerva—Latin meaning without inspiration or unwilling and literally "Minerva unwilling," that is without inspiration from the goddess of wisdom Minerva

Iolaus—in Greek mythology, Iolaus was a Theban divine hero famed for being Heracles's nephew, being one of the Argonauts and father of the mythic and historic kings of Corinth

Ipecac—an emetic made from dried roots

Ipil—a fast growing tropical tree of the legume family

Ipso facto—as the result of a particular fact, because of fact

Ironmongery—dealing in articles made of metal, a dealer in metal goods

Irredentism—the policy of advocating the restoration of territory formerly belonging to a country

Irredentist—an advocate, advocator, exponent or proponent, a person who pleads for a cause or propounds an idea; in the 1800s, Italian advocates for recovery of territory once a part of Italy

Irrefragable—impossible to refute or controvert, indisputable as in irrefragable evidence

Irremeable—admitting no return, permitting no return to the original place or condition, irreversible

Iser—Wolfgang Iser is known for his reader-response literary theory in which meaning is not an object within text but rather an event of construction that occurs somewhere between the text and the reader

Isinglass—a translucent gelatin made from fish bladders used as a clarifying agent in adhesives

Isomorphtic—having the same form or appearance as another thing

Isonomy—equality of civil or political rights, equality before the law

Isoperimetric—in mathematics, a geometric inequality that involves the surface area of a set and its volume

Isotropic—an object or substance having a physical property that has the same value when measured in different directions

Ispaghula—a Southern Asia plant that swells in water; in medicine, it is used because its swelling creates bulk that promotes movement and prevents constipation

Iterate—to say or do the same thing again, to repeat something; cf. reiterate

Ithyphallic—having an erect penis, upright

Itys—in mythology, Itys was the son of Tereus who Procne killed and served to Tereus at a banquet in revenge

Ius naturale—laws common to all beings and generally accepted by all, laws that make sense to reasonable people and are thus followed; cf. lumen naturale

J

Jack Tar—a common English term used to refer to seamen of the Merchant or Royal Navy; a sailor

Jade—an old horse that is worn out through overwork; an offensive term for a woman that insults her temperament or morality

Jalap—a twining plant native to Mexico with purgative powers

Jalousie—a blind or shutter made of a row of angled slats

Janus-faced— two-faced, being one thing and presenting another image to others

Jape—an adventure, escapade, lark or jaunt; a joke or act of mischief

Jasmine—a climbing fragrant plant often used in gardens; a perfume made from the oil of jasmine

Jasper—an opaque impure mineral of the variety silica, usually red, yellow, brown or green and rarely blue, used in ornamentation on items like vases and seals

Jeat—obsolete spelling for jet

Jejunum—the middle section of the small intestine whose main function is the absorption of nutrients

Jerboa—a small nocturnal rodent with large ears, long tail and hind legs for leaping native to Asia and Africa

Jeremiad—a long recitation of complaints, a lengthy complaint

Jeremiah—persecuted Hebrew religious prophet who revealed the people's sins and explained the reasons for their impending disaster

Jerkin—a sleeveless coat; a man's close-fitting tunic often made of leather in the sixteenth and seventeenth centuries

Jesuitical—of or concerning the Jesuits

Jib—the small triangular sail in front of the main sail on a sailing ship; the projecting arm of a crane; to stop and refuse to move; to be reluctant to do something

Jocund—to be jolly and full of good humor, jolly

Jointure—an estate or property settled by a husband with his wife at marriage to take effect upon his death

Jominian—pertaining to Antoine Henri Jomini, an early 1800s Swiss, French and Russian general and military tactician who wrote *Traité de Grande Tactique* in which his prescription for success was to put superior combat power at the decisive point

Judder—to shake violently; a violent, rapid vibration or shaking motion

Judenrein—from which Jews are excluded, originally from Nazi Germany

Julep—same as a mint julep, an alcoholic drink with mint garnish

Juno—in Roman mythology, the queen of the Gods; a woman of queenly bearing and imposing beauty

Junto—same as junta, a group of military officers who have taken control after a coup d'état

K

Kale—a hardy cabbage with dark green leaves and no heart; the same as money

Keen—intense and lively; having a sharp cutting edge; cold and penetrating (like a keen shriek); to make a loud, long sad sound, especially because someone has died

Keep—the strongest or central tower of a castle acting as the final place of refuge

Kenosis—the partial relinquishing of divinity like Jesus Christ's partly giving up divine status to become a man

Képis—a French military hat with a round flat top and visor

Key of Solomon—a seal used as a symbol for writing amulets and talismans used for exorcism or summoning daemons

Kindle—to begin to glow

Kine—archaic for cows or cattle

Kinked—a sudden spasm in a muscle, especially a crick in the neck

Kirk—the Church of Scotland, the largest Presbyterian church in Scotland

Kirsch—a clear, colorless fruit brandy traditionally made from cherries

Kitchen—anything spread on bread

Kleptocracy—a government where those in power exploit natural resources and steal, rule by thieves

Knave—a man who is considered dishonest and deceitful; a man who works as a servant

Knobkerrie—a form of club used mainly in Southern and Eastern Africa

Knout—a leather whip used for flogging; to beat somebody with a knout

Koinonia—Greek for communion, joint participation

Konak—a large house or mansion in the former Ottoman Empire

Korybant—a group of crested male dancers who worshiped the Phrygian goddess Cybele with drumming and dancing

Kptlt—an abbreviation for the military rank of captain-lieutenant such as in the German or English armed forces

Kraal—a traditional rural village surrounded by a stockade

Krishna—a major deity in Hinduism, the popular god of compassion, tenderness and love

Kumquat—a small oval orange fruit related to citrus fruits with sweet skin and tart flesh

Kvass—a fermented drink, low in alcohol, made from rye flour or bread with malt

L

La Noche Oscura—meaning "the dark night," a poetry book by Ecuadorean writer Alejandro Carrión

Laager—a camp protected by a circle of wagons used by the Boers in South Africa

Lachrymatory—a small bottle found in ancient tombs thought to contain the tears of mourners

Lacing—a small amount of alcohol added to a drink or food; a beating or thrashing

Lacrimation—the production of tears in the eyes, especially excessive production

Laibon—a medicine man

Laird—in Scotland, the owner of land, especially a large estate

Lamarck—Jean Baptiste Lamarck was a naturalist who proposed that species changed into new species based on use, e.g. giraffes that continually stretched their necks to reach leaves would select for longer necks

Lamarckian—or Lamarckian inheritance, the hypothesis that an organism can pass on characteristics that it has acquired in its lifetime to its offspring

Lamasery—a Tibetan monastery of lamas

Landanum—various preparations containing opium, a tincture of opium

Landau—a four-wheeled carriage with front and back passenger seats that face each other

Landes—an infertile moor; the sandy barren area boarding the sea in southwestern France

Landsturm—a general draft for conscription into the military; a military force consisting of people drafted through landsturm from the general population

Langouste—a spiny lobster

Languor—a pleasant feeling of weariness or weakness; listless and indifferent behavior; an oppressive heaviness in the air

Lapidary—engraved in stone or on a gemstone; relating to the art of cutting or engraving gemstones; careful, elegant and dignified in style

Lapis lazuli—or lapis for short, is a deep blue metamorphic rock used as a semi-precious stone that is prized for its intense color

Lapus linguo—Latin for an inadvertent error committed in talking, a lapse in language

Larboard—the port or left side of a vessel

Larder—a cool, usually small room or large cupboard used to store food; a supply of food

Larkspur—a delphinium plant with pink and white spiked flowers native to cool regions worldwide

Larme à l'oeil—French for "with tears in the eyes"

Lateen—a triangular sail attached to a mast or ship with such a sail

Lathe—a machine that rotates wood or metal while a cutting tool is applied to shape it

Lath—thin strips of wood used as framework to support other materials; a thin strip of wood often used in various building trades

Lation—a rare astronomical term meaning local motion from one place to another

Laudanum—a solution of opium in alcohol formerly used for pain relief

Lauds—in Catholicism the first prayer of seven separate canonical hours set aside for prayer each day, the morning prayer; in time around three a.m.; cf. Matins, Prime, Vespers, Compline

Laver—a Jewish ceremonial basin for washing; a washbasin

Lave—to wash

Lavoisier—an eighteenth-century French nobleman and chemist who revolutionized chemistry with his discovery of carbon, hydrogen and oxygen as well as oxygen's role in combustion, considered the father of modern chemistry

Layette—all things you need to know for a new baby, especially clothes

Lazar house—a leper colony or leprosarium, a place to quarantine people with leprosy

Lazaret—a small compartment below deck in the aft end of a vessel used for stores

Lazarus—from the Bible, Mary's brother and a friend of Jesus who died but was brought to life again by Jesus; a man restored to life by Jesus Christ or figuratively by faith

Lebensraum—space required for life, growth and activity; territory believed necessary for national existence and economic self-sufficiency, especially by Nazis

Lectionary—a book that contains a collection of scripture readings in Christian or Judaic religions

Lecton—an abstraction or something with just nominal existence, like space and time

Leek—an edible plant with green leaves related to the onion

Lees—the remains, residue, sediment, silt or deposit

Leeward—the side sheltered from the wind, downwind; cf. windward

Legerdemain—sleight of hand; skill or cleverness, especially for deceitful purposes

Lemma—in logic, a proposition that is assumed to be true in order to test the validity of another proposition; a heading that indicates the topic of a work; a term that is defined in a glossary

Lenitive—capable of easing pain or discomfort, e.g. a lenitive medicine

Lenity—the state or quality of being lenient, clemency, as in lenity in a sentence

Lenten—relating to Lent

Leonine—characteristic of a lion, lion like

Leprous—having or relating to leprosy; resembling the physical symptoms of leprosy, especially being pale or scaly

Lèse magesté—the crime of violating majesty, an offense against the dignity of a sovereign or the state

Lese-majesty—to insult a monarch or other ruler, treason

Lesseps statue—a bronze statue of Ferdinand de Lesseps, who was a French diplomat and developer of the Suez Canal, located at the entrance to the canal, destroyed by Egyptian resistance in 1956 but rebuilt

Lestrygonian—in Greek mythology, a tribe of man-eating giants that inhabited southeast Sicily described by Polybius and Thucydides

Lethe—in Greek mythology, a river in Hades whose water made those who drank it forget their past, the forgetfulness river of Hades

Letter of Marque—a letter licensing reprisal from a government to privateers to attack and capture enemy vessels

Lettuce—paper money as opposed to coins; cf. obolus

Leukos—white

Levantine— a rich, heavy twilled silk cloth, silk fabric

Levant—to leave secretly or hurriedly to avoid paying debts; geographically, the countries along the eastern Mediterranean shores (modern-day Turkey, Syria and Lebanon)

Levée en masse—the mass conscription of Frenchmen for service in the Revolutionary War; a short-term requisition of all able-bodied men to defend a nation

Levée—an embankment built to prevent the overflow of a river; a ridge of sediment deposited naturally alongside a river; a landing place, a quay

Leveret—a young hare, especially one less than a year old

Levin—lightning, thunderbolts

Levite—a member of the tribe of Levi, a priestly tribe chosen to assist the priests of the Jewish Temple

Levy—to impose a tax; to enlist troops for military service; to seize property to fulfill a judgment

Leyden jar—an early device for condensing static electricity consisting of a glass jar, metal foil and a rod passing through it

Liana—a woody climbing tropical vine

Libidinous—having excessive sexual drive, lustful

Licit—allowed by law, lawful; cf. illicit

Lickerish—taking an excessive or unfair amount without concern for others, greedy; continually thinking about sex or trying to make sexual contact with others, lecherous

Ligature—something used for binding or tying things together; a unifying link or bond

Lighter—a flat-bottomed open cargo boat used primarily to transport goods from a large vessel to port

Lilt—a pleasant rising and falling variation in a person's voice; a bouncy way of walking; a cheerful song, especially one easy to sing along with

Limber—a two-wheeled detachable vehicle that is the front part of a gun carriage used for transporting ammunition, a vehicle for transporting a large gun

Lime—in the Caribbean, to spend time lazily; to cover a surface with whitewash

Limes—to paint a surface with whitewash; the color lime green; in the Caribbean to laze about, be lazy

Linden—a deciduous tree of temperate regions with cordate leaves

Lingua franca—a language that is adopted as a common language between speakers of different languages

Linnaean system—a biologic taxonomic system created by Carl Linnaeus

Linstock—a long staff with a forked end designed to hold a lighted match used to fire cannons

Lintel—a horizontal beam that supports the weight of the wall above a window or door

Linthead—a deregulatory term for a mill hand

Lint—short, fine fibers that separate from the surface of cloth during processing; the fibrous material of a cotton boll

Lipothymia—fainting or a feeling of fainting, swooning

Liripipe—the long tail hanging from the back of an academic hood

Lisp—to speak in a childish or halting way

List—historically, the barriers enclosing an area for a jousting tournament

Litharge—from Greek meaning silver stone, a natural mineral that forms lead

Litotes—a deliberate understatement often expressed negatively such as "not a bad actor" or "not unhappy"

Littoral—the area on or near a shore, especially the zone between low and high tides

Livery—an identifying uniform worn by a group or trade; distinctive coloring, marking, dress or outward appearance; the care, feeding and stabling of horses for money

Livity—the Rastafarian concept of righteousness, essentially an energy force conferred by God that exists within all people; cf. Rastafarian

Lochinvar—a fictional, brave and romantic character by Sir Walter Scott who boldly takes his love Ellen at her wedding

Loess—a fine-grained soil often left by the wind

Loggia—a covered, open-sided walkway along the side of a building; a balcony in a theater

Logique—logical; cf. espagnolisme

Logogram—a symbol that represents the meaning of a word or phrase, e.g. using "&" instead of "and"; cf. acrophonic

Logography—a method of longhand reporting by writing down few words; historically, the use of logotypes in printing

Logotherapy—a directive existential psychotherapy that emphasizes the importance of meaning in the patient's life especially gained through spiritual values

Loin—the area on each side of the backbone between the ribs and hips; tender meat cut from the backbone and rib areas; cf. sirloin

Lollard—fourteenth-century preachers (and movement) that stirred riots by the virulence of their preaching against the friars

Long in tooth—old, especially of horses and people; extending a considerable distance; lasting for an extended period of time; extended beyond what is considered normal; possessing more than is enough of something

Longobards—another term for the ancient Lombards who were a Germanic people who ruled most of the Italian Peninsula during the sixth through eighth centuries

Lorgnette—a pair of glasses held to the eyes or by a short handle on one side

Lorgnon—eyeglasses, especially opera eyeglasses

Lough—same as lake; a long inlet of the sea

Loupe—a magnifying glass used especially by jewelers and watchmakers

Lour—another spelling of lower or lowery; to lower; obsolete meaning is dull or stupid

Lowing—the deep sound characteristic of animals like cows and oxen

Lozenge—a diamond-shaped figure, a rhombus or diamond shape; a diamond-shaped design on heraldic arms

Lubberland—a fictional land of the clumsy, stupid, loutish, fat and lazy Cockaigne that abounds with luxury, sexual liberty and plentiful food

Lubricity—behavior that is obscene, unchaste or lewd

Lucida—in astronomy, the brightest star in the constellation

Lucubration—a written work resulting from long study that is often scholarly; long hard study, especially at night

Ludicrous—so foolish, unreasonable or out of place to be amusing or ridiculous

Luff—to sail too close to the wind so the sails flap; the front edge of a sail

Lulli— Giovanni Battista Lulli (1632–1687) was a French composer in the court of Louis XIV who founded the national French opera; cf. Rameau

Lumbago—a medical term for lower back pain the exact cause of which is unknown

Lumen naturale—in medieval philosophy and theology, ordinary cognitive powers of human reason unaided by supernatural light of grace or divine revelation; cf. ius naturale

Lumen natural—lumen is a measure of the total quantity of visible light emitted by a source, lumen natural is such a light from a natural source

Lumen—the space inside any tubular structure in the body such as an intestine or artery; the cavity within a plant cell wall

Lumpen—living on the margins of society; stupidly content with a life intellectually empty and socially inferior

Lure—a device swung to attract or recall a falcon, usually consisting of a line and leather bag

Lurid—presented in vivid, shocking and sensational terms, especially in sexual and criminal matters; very vivid in color, especially when creating harsh or unnatural effects

Lustration—to make somebody spiritually pure through a religious ceremony

Lustrine—a glossy silk fabric, or satin-weave fabric resembling it

Lusus naturae—a freak of nature; a mutant, variant or freak; a deformed monster, anomaly

Lycanthropy—the supernatural transformation of a person into a wolf, as recounted in folk tales; a form of madness involving the delusion of being an animal, usually a wolf

Lyddite—a powerful explosive consisting of picric acid and petroleum jelly

Lysis—the disintegration of a cell by rupture of the cell wall or membrane

M

Macaque—a short-tailed monkey native to Asia and North Africa

Macaronic—burlesque verse that contains words or inflections from another language; verse that mixes vernacular with Latin

Machen—to take part in, to participate

Machicolation—a projecting gallery on the top of a castle wall supported by arches used to throw rocks and boiling oil on attackers

Macula peccati—the stain of the original sin

Macula—a small pigmented spot on the skin; a small yellowish spot in the retina that provides visual acuity and color perception; a sunspot

Maculate—to mark somebody or something with a spot, blotch or blemish; marked with spots, blotches or blemishes

Maculation—the pattern of spots on some animals and plants; the act of marking something with a spot, blotch or blemish

Madder—a herb of the madder family with whorled leaves, small yellowish flowers and dark berries

Maecenas—a Roman statesman and friend and patron of Horace and Virgil; a rich patron of the arts; a noun that determines reality by naming people, objects, sensations, feelings, etc.

Magellanic—characteristic of the Strait of Magellan or that general area of the southern hemisphere; the Magellanic Cloud of the Milky Way Galaxy, which is a vast star system of which Earth is a minor component

Magenta—a brilliant purplish pink color

Magi—in the Bible, the Three Wise Men who came to Bethlehem from the East to celebrate the birth of Jesus Christ

Maidan—in South Asia, open space where games are played and meetings are held

Maieutic—in philosophy, the same as Socratic or Socrates philosophy and particularly his method of arriving at the truth; a student or follower of Socrates

Major-domo—the chief steward of a large household; cf. chatelaine

Mala fide—in bad faith, such as a purchaser who acts in bad faith when they know the property has been stolen; cf. bona fide

Malacca—a walking stick made from rattan

Maladorous—smelling very unpleasant

Malapropos—French for inappropriate, out of place, inopportune, untimely as in a malapropos remark

Malediction—a curse; slander or evil talk about somebody

Maleficiam—Latin meaning wrongdoing or mischief; describes malevolent or harmful magic, evildoing; generally any magical act intended to cause harm to others

Mall—also known as pall-mall, a seventeenth-century game in which each player attempts to drive a wooden ball with a mallet down an alley and through a raised ring in as few strokes as possible

Mallow—a plant with fine hairs on its stem and leaves and disc-shaped fruit

Malmsey—a fortified Madeira wine of the sweetest type

Malversate—to fraudulently appropriate for one's own use, to embezzle or peculate

Malversation—dishonest or unethical conduct by a professional or public official often involving bribery, extortion or embezzlement

Mameluke—a member of a former military caste originally comprising enslaved Turks that ruled Egypt between the thirteenth and sixteenth centuries

Mammock—a small piece of something; to tear something up to shreds

Mamre—in Hebrew tradition, an ancient shrine originally focused on a single holy tree belonging to Canaan

Mamur—a prefect or governor

Mana—power, effectiveness and prestige, usually from a supernatural, inexplicable source

Mandala—a geometric or pictorial design usually enclosed in a circle representing the entire universe used in meditation in Buddhism and Hinduism; in Jungian psychology, a symbol representing the self and inner harmony

Mandrake root—thought to be a magical plant used in spells and rituals, the root was thought to scream when it is dug up, killing everyone who heard its cries

Manelchen—Immanuel Kant's mother nicknamed him Manelchen, which roughly translates to "little Manny"

Mange—an infectious skin disease of animals and sometimes humans caused by mites that result in hair loss, scabs and itching

Manna—according to the Bible, food God gave the Israelites in the desert after escaping from Egypt

Manse— the house occupied by a minister of a Presbyterian church

Mantelet—a woman's short, loose sleeveless cloak or shawl; a bulletproof screen for a solider

Mantic—having the powers of divination or prophecy

Manticratic—rule by the family or clan of a prophet, a neologism coined by T. E. Lawrence in *The Seven Pillars of Wisdom*

Mantram—a word or sound repeated to aid concentration in meditation; a statement or slogan repeated frequently

Mantua—a woman's gown with an open front and draped skirt to show the underskirt popular in Europe in the late seventeenth and eighteenth centuries

Manufactory—a factory

Marabout—an administrator of poor relief

Marasma—severe malnutrition characterized by lack of energy

Marchese—an Italian marquis

Marchioness—in the United Kingdom, a noblewoman who ranks below a duchess and above a countess; the wife or widow of a marquess

Margrave—a German nobleman equivalent to a British marquess

Mariolatry—in Christianity, extreme devotion to Mary the mother of Jesus

Mariposa—a bulbous plant of the lily family with brightly colored tulip-shaped flowers

Marmoreal—made of marble or like marble; figuratively being white, cold, aloof and impressive

Marplot—an officious meddler whose interference compromises the success of an undertaking

Marque—a brand or make of product

Marquee—a permanent canopy protecting the entrance to a building like a hotel; having public appeal or considered in connection with the public, as in a committee with a star has great marquee value

Marquess—a British nobleman ranking above an earl and below a duke

Marquetry—designs or pictures made of thin wood, metal or other material inlaid in a wood veneer used for decorating furniture

Marquis—a British nobleman ranking above an earl and below a duke

Marquise—a noblewoman ranking above a countess or the wife of a marquis; cf. countess, duchess

Marse—Southern America slang for master

Mary Magdalene—a Jewish woman who witnessed Jesus's crucifixion and resurrection characterized by various religions as a saint, a heroine of faith, promiscuous woman or a prostitute

Marzipan—a sweet paste made of ground almonds, sugar and egg yolks used to mold cakes

Massif—a large mountain mass; a part of the Earth's crust surrounded by faults that may be displaced by tectonic movements

Mathesis—a branch of philosophy involving the ordering of simple natures that can be studied quantitatively

Matinal—relating to matins or taking place during matins; cf. matins

Matins—in the Roman Catholic Church, the morning hours of the divine office; the ceremony of morning prayer; a morning song, especially one sung by birds

Matins—time around midnight; cf. Lauds, Prime, Vespers, Compile

Matzah—a thin, crisp unleavened bread traditionally eaten by Jews during Passover

Matzo—same as matzah, unleavened bread traditionally eaten during Passover

Mauve—light or pale purple, lavender, violet

Maya—broadly illusion; the supernatural power of gods to produce illusions; the power by which the universe becomes manifest; the illusion of appearance of the phenomenal world

Mayhap—maybe, perhaps, possibly, something that may happen

Mazipan—a sweet, yellowish paste of ground almonds, sugar and egg whites used to make small cakes or as icing, also called almond paste

Mea culpa—Latin for "through my fault" or an acknowledgement of having done wrong

Meagre—unsatisfactory in quantity or size, small; of bad or unsatisfying quality; very thin, especially through malnutrition or illness

Mealie—Indian corn

Mealy—powdery or granular, like meal or grain; having a spotted or dappled hide or coat; exceptionally pale, especially through malnutrition or illness

Meatus—a passage or opening leading to the interior of the body; cf. orificium urethrae

Meconium—the dark greenish feces that collect in the intestines of an unborn baby and are released shortly after birth, the first feces of a newborn baby

Mediate—to be between two stages, ideas, times or things

Mediumistic—the practice of mediums who purport to mediate between spirits of the dead and living human beings

Medlar—a small apple-shaped fruit; a tree with apple-shaped fruit

Meerschaum—a fine whitish mineral like clay; a tobacco pipe with a bowl made of meerschaum

Megarian—in philosophy, an adherent of Socrates moral philosophy, named after Euclid of Megara was a disciple of Socrates

Megrim—same as a migraine; a sudden change of mind about something that was formerly enthusiastically embraced

Mein—my or mine in German

Mélange—a collection of things of different kinds

Melanism—dark pigmentation of the skin or hair of a human being due to the presence of melanin

Meleager—in Greek mythology, the son of Althaea who the Fates said would live only as long as a piece of wood, burning, remained unconsumed; Althaea then stole the branch and kept it safe; later Meleager killed his uncles, so Althaea burned the branch and Meleager died

Melopoeia—when words are charged beyond their normal meaning with some musical property; inducing emotional correlations by sound and rhythm through speech

Melusine—a female spirit of fresh water in a sacred spring or river usually depicted as a fish from the waist down like a mermaid

Meme—a cultural characteristic such as language that can be transmitted from generation to generation like the transmission of genetic information

Memetic—a unit of culture such as an idea or belief that individuals carry that can reproduce itself thereby jumping from mind to mind

Mene—mysterious words written on a wall of Belshazzar's palace predicting the doom of the king and his dynasty

Meninge—same as meningo or meningococcal disease or meningitis, a serious viral infectious disease

Meningioma— a slow-growing benign tumor that affects the brain or spinal cord that may cause damage due to pressure

Menses—menstruation or the period it lasts; the blood and other matter during menstruation

Mensuration—the calculation of geometric qualities such as length, area and volume from dimensions and angles already known; the act of measuring something

Mercer—in the United Kingdom, a dealer in silks and other fine cloth, a dealer in fine textiles

Meridian—the peak or a high point, such as in development or success; in geography, an imaginary line between the North and South Poles that crosses the equator at a right angle

Merino—a sheep belonging to a breed originally developed in Spain that is raised for its wool; the long fine white wool of the merino sheep

Mésalliance—a mismatched marriage due to the lower social position of one partner

Mesmerism—a popular hoax theory in the eighteenth century perpetrated by German Franz Mesmer that claimed invisible fluid around every object that could be manipulated to cure disease and bring moral health

Mesomorph—a husky, muscular body; cf. ectomorph, endomorph

Mesomorphic—a person with a husky, muscular body; cf. ectomorphic, endomorphic

Mesozoic—the Mesozoic Era was the age of reptiles when dinosaurs flourished and went extinct and mammals, birds and flowering plants appeared for the first time

Metamorphic—in geology, a rock that has undergone transformation by heat, pressure or other natural processes; marked by metamorphosis

Metanoia—Greek for a transformative change of heart, especially a spiritual conversion; a repudiation, change of mind, repentance or atonement; a reformation

Metaphrase—a word for word literal translation of something

Metastasis—the migration of cancer from site to another

Metempsychosis—a supposed transmigration at death of the soul of a human to a new body

Meteorism—a medical condition where excess gas accumulates in the gastrointestinal tract causing distention, also known as tympanites

Metic—in ancient Greece, an alien having some rights of citizenship

Metonymy—a figure of speech in which an attribute of something is used to stand for the thing itself, e.g. "laurels" for "glory"; cf. synecdoche

Metronome—a device used to indicate tempo by means of a regular signal, a device to mark time

Mew—a gull; a cage for hawks; to confine a hawk or falcon by tying it to a perch

Mewe—German for a town on the Vistula River in Poland

Mewl—to whimper like a cat

Mezzotint—an engraving process that involves treating the surface of a copper plate; print produced by the mezzotint process

Midden—a pile of dung or refuse, a dunghill

Milch—producing milk

Millare—a miller, one that operates a mill

Millet—the shiny grain of a cereal plant used for flour and alcoholic drinks; a fast growing cereal plant

Milliard—one thousand million, a billion

Millsick—a machine that reduces a solid substance into pulp by crushing, grinding or pressing; a building with machinery for processing raw materials into finished products, e.g. a textile or steel mill

Mimeos—a mimeograph, to make a replica, copy or drawing or recreate a picture

Mimosa—an Australian acacia tree with delicate leaves and yellow flowers; another name for the silk tree; a drink of champagne and orange juice

Minerva—in Roman mythology, the goddess of wisdom and patron of the arts, trade and the art of war

Minima—plural of minimum

Minish—to make less, fewer in number, diminish in power or influence, to lessen

Miniver—a white fur used as trim on ceremonial costumes

Minx—a young woman who is pert, flirtatious or imprudent; a promiscuous woman

Miry—marshy ground or slushy mud, a bog; thick slimy mud; a troublesome or oppressive situation difficult to escape

Mise en abîme—a French phrase derived from heraldry that literally means "placed into an abyss" that has taken on additional meanings such as an image that contains a smaller copy of itself

Mise-en-scène—the positioning of actors, scenery and properties on a stage or movie set

Misprision—the failure to report a crime to authorities; wrongdoing by a public official in the performance of their duties; sedition against the government or a court

Misprize—to fail to appreciate the worth of something, to undervalue; to consider something or somebody unworthy of admiration

Miter—a Christian bishop's ceremonial hat with a tall, pointed crease across the top and two ribbons hanging down the back

Mithridate—in ancient medicine, a substance believed to be an antidote to every poison and cure for every disease

Mitsein—from Heidegger's phenomenological philosophy, the feature of being with others, which is essential to being human

Mobocracy—political control by the mob, control by the mob; a place where the mob has political control

Mobocrat—a member of the mob who exercise political control; cf. mobocracy

Modillion—a small, curved ornamental bracket under the corona of a Corinthian column

Modish—conforming to the latest fashions, styles or fads, to be fashionable

Modus vivendi—a feasible arrangement or compromise that avoids disagreement

Moiety—one of two parts into which something can be divided; societies that consist of two halves for ritual or marriage purposes and where marriages may be forbidden within the same moiety

Moiling—a state of agitation or confusion; hard work, drudgery

Moil—to work hard, drudge; to be in agitation and confusion

Monarchien—German for monarchies

Monition—a warning, especially of danger; advice urging caution; in law, an order to appear at court, a summons

Monkshood—a poisonous purplish perennial plant native to Europe

Monodies—in Greek tragedy, an ode for one actor to sing alone; in poetry a poem that mourns somebody's death

Monody—an ode sung by a single actor in Greek tragedy; a poem lamenting a person's death

Monogamy—the custom of being married to only one person at a time; having one sexual partner; cf. exogamy, endogamy, polyandry, polygamy

Monstrance—a large gold or silver container for consecrated bread in Rome

Moor—a large, uncultivated, treeless stretch of land covered with bracken heather, coarse grasses or moss

Morbidities—in epidemiology, the prevalence of a disease in a particular percentage of the population, the number of cases of a particular disease per unit of population

Mordant—sarcastic or scathingly critical; having a corrosive effect; an acid used in etching a metal plate in printing

Morganatic—a marriage where the socially lower ranked spouse or their children do not inherit property of the socially higher ranking spouse; marriage between people of different social ranks

Morisco—Islamic Moors in Christian Spain in the sixteenth century

Morpheme—the smallest meaningful element of speech or writing

Morphodite—slang for hermaphrodite or an organism that has both male and female organs often considered offensive

Mortmain—in law, the perpetual, inalienable ownership of real estate by a corporation or legal institution

Mos maiorum—Latin for ancestral custom, way of the elders or ancestral custom, a core concept in ancient Rome

Mote—a tiny particle or speck

Motet—a short piece of sacred choral music, typically polyphonic and unaccompanied

Mottetto—a vocal musical composition of highly diverse form and style from the late medieval period

Mottoe—a brief statement used to express a principle, goal or ideal

Mouser—a domestic animal that catches mice, especially a cat

Moxa—a cone or cylinder of downy material derived from plants used to balm skin burns

Muezzin—a man who calls Muslims to prayer

Muffle—to wrap or cover for warmth

Muggle—a person who is not good at a particular activity or skill

Mull—to heat, sweeten and flavor with spices for drinking as with ale or wine

Mullion— a vertical bar between the panes of a glass in a window; cf. transom

Mummer—somebody who celebrates wearing a mask; a actor or mime; a house serf; cf. mummery

Mummery—a performance by mummers; a showy or hypocritical ceremony; cf. mummer

Mundane—relating to matters of this world, of this world

Murrian—Richard Murrian was a Paris-based American photographer known for his photography of girls

Murther—same as murder

Muslin—a cotton fabric of plain weave often with patterns and used in sheets

Must—the juice from grapes or fruit that is to be fermented into wine, unfermented grape

Mutatis mutandis—Latin meaning with the necessary changes having been made, or including changes

Muzak—recorded light background music played in public places

Muzhik—a Russian peasant, especially during the Tsarist era

Myriad—a countless or extremely large number; in classical history, ten thousand, which was the highest number in Greek arithmetic

Myrrh—an aromatic resinous gum from various trees and bushes in Africa used in perfume, incense and medicine

Mysterium Coniunctionis—a book by Carl Jung in which he synthesized the opposites in alchemy and psychology

Mysto—an abbreviation for mystical

Myth of Horus—Horus was an early Egyptian god portrayed as a hawk or falcon and worshiped as a sun god and creator of the sky

Mythologem—a basic or recurrent theme of myth such as the universal flood

Mythomanic—the inclination to alter the truth, exaggerate or tell lies

Mythopoeic—the making of a myth or myths

Mythos—the set of beliefs, attitudes and values held by a society

N

Nabob—a person of conspicuous wealth or high status; a person who returned from India to Europe with a fortune; a Muslim official or governor under the Mogul empire

Naif—a naïve or inexperienced person

Nankeen—a durable yellowish-brown cotton fabric

Nape—the back part of the neck

Naphtha—a clear colorless flammable mixture of hydrocarbons used in plastics

Napped—the surface of a piece of cloth whose short threads have been brushed in one direction

Nappie—an absorbent material wrapped around a baby's bottom to absorb urine and feces; a diaper

Nap—the short fuzzy ends of fibers on the surface of cloth

Narcolepsy—a condition of uncontrollable bouts of deep sleep sometimes accompanied by hallucinations and immobility

Nard—same as spikenard, a perennial aromatic plant native to the Himalayan range; a fragrant ointment derived from spikenard used in ancient times

Narwhal—a small arctic whale with a spotted body and short flippers

Natty—a person or article of clothing that is smart and fashionable

Natura naturans—Latin meaning nature naturing or nature doing what nature does; cf. natura naturata

Natura naturata—Latin meaning having natured or nature already created; cf. natura naturans

Nauarchy—a high office in ancient Sparta

Nautch—in India, a dance by women designed for the erotic entertainment for men

Nave—the central isle or main body of a church, cf. chancel

Neapolitan—relating to Naples; a citizen of Naples

Nebbish—an offensive term that insults somebody's courage and personality

Nebulae—clouds of interstellar dust or gas appearing as hazy bright or dark patches, space dust

Nebulosity—same as nebula, a region of space gas occasionally appearing as a hazy bright patch; figuratively, something hazy appearing occasionally; capricious and vague

Neem—a tall evergreen tree grown for its bark, resin and seed oil, which have medicinal and insecticidal properties, native to Asia

Née—the maiden name of a woman; introducing the name of something that was formally known as something else

Neologism—the invention of a new word

Neoplasm—a tumor or tissue containing a growth

Nervure—a supporting structure resembling a rod that is visible inside an insect's wing

Nescience—lack of knowledge or awareness, ignorance

Nessum dorma—Italian for "none shall sleep," which is the final act of an opera by Glacomo Puccini

Neurasthenia—nervous exhaustion

Neurasthenic—describing a condition of chronic mental and physical fatigue and depression

Nevertheless—in spite of that, despite a situation or comment

Newel—a post supporting the handrail of a staircase at the top or bottom

Newgate calendar—a popular eighteenth- and nineteenth-century book originally citing executions and the most notorious criminals from the 1700s produced by the keeper of the Newgate prison in London

Newser—a news conference

Ni roi, ni loi—neither king, law or faith

Nib—a sharp point or tip; the metal tip of a pen, especially a quill pen; same as beak

Nibbed—made a sharp point; cf. nib

Nihil obstat—Latin meaning nothing hinders or nothing stands in the way, a declaration of no objection to something

Nil desperandum—Latin meaning nothing must be despaired, never despair

Nimbus—a halo or disc around the head; a surrounding aura of splendor

Nine-pins—very formally or elaborately dressed

Niobe—in Greek mythology, the daughter of Tantalus who was punished by the gods for claiming superiority over their mother Leto; her children were killed, and she was turned into stone

Nirdvandva—freedom from oppression

Nirvanic—like paradise or heaven

Nisse—in Scandinavian folklore, a household spirit responsible for the care and prosperity of a farm usually described as a short man

Niter—another term for potassium nitrate, a white crystalline salt used in fertilizer, meat preservatives and gunpowder, also known as saltpeter

Nob and swell—British words for stylish persons of wealth and high social position

Nocturnal—happening at night; cf. diurnal

Nocturns—in the Roman Catholic Church, a part of matins originally said at night; cf. matins

Noema—Greek for what is thought or thought about; cf. noematic, noesis, noetic

Noematic—pertaining to the understanding; relating to noema or thought or what is thought about; cf. noesis, noema, noesis, noetic

Noesis—intellect or intelligence, the functioning of the intellect, the exercise of reason; cf. noematic, noema, noetic

Noetic—pertaining to mental activity or the intellect; cf. noema, noematic, noesis

Nolle prosequ—a formal notice of abandonment of a plaintiff or prosecutor of all or part of a suit or action; cf. nol-prossed

Nolle—Latin meaning to not care to proceed; cf. velle

Nol-prossed—to abandon a suit by issuing a nolle prosequ; cf. nolle prosequ

Nominal—in philosophy, an accepted condition that is usually an approximation as opposed to something real

Nominalism—the philosophic view that denies universals and abstract objects; rather, they exist only in names

Nominative absolute—a grammatically independent element of a sentence realized as a noun phrase and a participle or adjective

Nominativus pendens—a normative case grammatically unconnected with the rest of the sentence in which it stands, a noun phrase introduced as the subject of a sentence that is not actually used as such; cf. nominative absolute

Nomology—the science of the laws of the mind

None—from Latin, nona or ninth, the ninth hour, a midafternoon prayer that is a fixed time of prayer

Nonplussed—to be surprised, confused or uncertain what to do or say; cool, calm, collected and unperturbed; cf. bemused

Noog—a bipedal terrestrial carnivore with an intimidating body stance

Noögenic—a neurosis stemming from existential frustration or crisis

Noölogical—relating to the mind or to mental character

Norn—an extinct language spoken in parts of northern Scotland; in Norse mythical goddesses representing the past, present and future who determines the destiny of gods and mortals

Nosegay—a small bouquet of flowers

Nosh—food; to eat food greedily

Nosography—the systematic description of diseases including symptoms and etiology

Nous—the mind or intellect; common sense or practical intelligence

Nova—a star that suddenly increases in brightness and then fades

Novena—in Catholicism, the recitation of prayer for nine days to achieve some purpose

Nubile—young and sexually desirable; a young woman physically mature enough for sexual intercourse and thus suitable for marriage

Nulius addictus inare in verba magistri—Latin for "be skeptical of the experts"

Numa—a village on Bougainville Island in the Solomon Islands

Numen—a spirit or divine power presiding over a thing or place

Numerology—the study of the occult use and supposed power of numbers

Numinosity—the inexpressible, mysterious, terrifying, directly experienced pertaining only to the divinity

Nunc dimittas—also known as the Song of Simeon from the New Testament meaning "now you dismiss" and often used as the final song in a religious service

Nuncio—an ecclesiastical diplomat

Nuptial—relating to weddings or marriage

Nymphomania—uncontrollable or excessive sexual desire in a woman; cf. satyriasis

O

O felix culpa—Latin for "O happy fault," philosophically, God allows evil because it brings a greater good

Obbligato—not to be omitted from a musical piece; in music, an essential part

Obiter dictum—in law, an observation by a judge that is incidental to the case that is not binding on future courts under the doctrine of precedent; a passing comment

Oblate—in a sphere, flattened at the poles, cf. prolate; a layman living in a monastery without vows; a member of one of several Roman Catholic communities of men or women

Oblateness—shaped like a sphere but oblique like an oval

Oblation—a thing presented or offered to God

Oblomovian—to be lazy and apathetic, which definition was derived from Goncharoy's 1859 novel *Oblomov* about a nobleman who rarely left his bed

Obol—an ancient Greek coin equal to one sixth of a drachma

Obolus—a coin used in ancient Greece; cf. lettuce

Obtrude—to impose something like one's opinions; to appear in a way that is unwelcome but cannot be ignored

Obverse—a counterpart or opposite; in logic, one proposition derived from another denying the first proposition, e.g. the obverse of "we are free" is "we are unfree"

Occident—the western hemisphere, especially countries in Europe and America; that part of the western sky where the sun sets

Occoquan—a historic town in Prince William County, Virginia which means in American Indian "at the end of the water"

Ocher—a reddish or yellowish earthy iron oxide used in pigment; a color that is yellow-brown and orangey

Ochlocracy—rule by the mob

Octant—in astronomy, the position of one body in the sky one-eighth of a circle, or forty-five degrees, from another

Octroi—a former local tax in some European countries levied on goods entering a town or city; in French, to grant

Oddment—something left over when most of something has been used, as in "odds and ends"; an odd thing

Oderint dum metuant—Latin for "let them hate me, so that they will but fear me," Caligula's motto

Odour—archiac for odor

Odred—French for detachment or separation

Oecist—a colonizer, particularly in ancient Greece

Oecologist—obsolete term for ecologist

Oecumenical—British spelling of ecumenical; cf. ecumenical; differences and relations between societies; cf. parochial

Oedipus complex—in psychoanalysis from Freud, a child's desire for their opposite-sex parent and resentment toward their same-sex parent

Oestrum—or estrus in zoology, a regularly occurring period of sexual receptivity

Oeuvre—a work of art or literature considered as a unit, especially the complete work of a single artist

Offal—the edible internal organs of an animal such as the heart, liver, brains and tongue, sometimes regarded as unpalatable; something discarded as refuse

Office—a task, assignment or chore; something said or done by someone for another person, e.g. I got the promotion through his kind office

Ogress—a female monster in fairy tales and legend usually represented as a hideous, ugly, cruel and barbarous giant woman who feeds on human flesh

Oiser—a species of willow or deciduous trees and shrubs

Oleaginous—containing or producing oil; similar to oil, oil-like; figuratively ingratiating, unpleasantly eager to please or charm

Oleograph—a colored, lithographic print made on canvass with oil colors in order to imitate an oil painting

Olive—a small oval bitter fruit with a pit that yields olive oil; olive green, a yellowish green color

Olla podrida—a traditional Spanish and Latin American stew of meat and vegetables

Omnia vincit labor improbus—Latin for "work or labor conquers all," from Virgil's *Georgics*

Omnibus—a volume containing several novels published previously separately; comprising several items

Omniseminous—the quality of being omniscient

Omnivorous—eating all types of foods including both plants and animals

Onanistic—the act of masturbating; same as coitus interruptus

Oncogene—an often mutated gene that has the potential to cause cancer

Oneiric—relating to or similar to dreams, in or like a dream

Ontic—of existence, relating to real existence

Onus probandi—in law, the general rule that the one who alleges shall prove it, the obligation to prove an assertion lays on the one who makes it, the burden of proof

Onyx—a fine-grained semiprecious stone with different color bands used in gems

Opéra bouffe—comic opera, usually with a happy ending

Opere-buffe—Italian for comic opera

Ophthalmic—relating to the eyes or region of the eyes

Oppilative—in medicine, a medicine that obstructs or closes the pores; to obstruct, obstructive

Optative—relating to the making of choices; in grammar, a mood that expresses wishes or desires

Opuscule—an insignificant creative piece of work, especially a musical or literary work

Orbis—a circle, orb, ring, disk or orbit

Orcus—the underworld

Ordinate—the vertical coordinate of a point on a two dimensional graph in which pairs of numbers denote distances along fixed horizontal and vertical axes, the vertical coordinate of a point

Oregeat—an extract of barley or almonds

Organon—a set of principles used in philosophical or scientific investigation

Orgōne—a universal life force; a cosmic unit of energy; the creative force in nature

Oriel extension—a window that extends beyond the face of a building over the public right of way

Orificium urethrae—the external opening of the urethra where urine exits the body; cf. meatus

Oriflamme—a red banner or flag that was the national flag of France in the Middle Ages

Origenism—the doctrines of third-century Christian theologian Origen whose Christian philosophy was based on the scriptures and Platonism

Originaliter—originally

Orison—a prayer or plea to a deity, a prayer

Ormolu—a gold-colored alloy of copper cast into desired shapes and often guided used in the eighteenth century for decorating furniture and ornaments

Orohydrographical—a branch of hydrography that deals with the relations of mountains to drainage

Orpheus—in Greek mythology a poet or musician who descended to the underworld to seek his wife Eurydice after her death but failed to bring her back

Orpiment—a bright yellow arsenic sulfide material used in dyeing and tanning

Orrery—a model of the solar system

Orthographic—related to the study of spelling; correct in spelling

Orthography—the study of correct spelling; the study of letters of an alphabet and their arrangement; the way letters and diacritic symbols represent the sounds of a language in spelling

Orthostatic—relating to or caused by standing in an upright position, associated with standing upright

Osier—a willow tree with long flexible stems used in making baskets and furniture; a willow branch or tree

Ossuary—an urn or vault used to hold the bones of the dead

Ostler—another spelling for hostler, somebody that services a large vehicle or machine like a locomotive or crane, and engineer; somebody who takes care of horses at an inn

Otiose—serving no practical purpose; indolent, idle; cf. otiosity

Otiosity—noun form of otiose; cf. otiose

Ouachita—a river running through northeast Arkansas and Louisiana to the Red River

Oubliette—a secret dungeon with access only through a trapdoor in its ceiling

Outrée—unusual and startling, weird, queer or outlandish, peculiarly or shockingly unusual, unconventional or bizarre

Over-weening—showing excessive confidence or pride

Ovolo—in architecture, a round convex molding, in a cross section, a quarter of a circle

Oxbridge—in England the universities of Oxford and Cambridge combined

P

Padawan—an apprentice, also known as a Padawan learner

Paddock—a small field near a house or stable for grazing horses; the area near the pits on a racetrack where cars are worked on before a race

Paella—a Spanish rice dish with chicken, chorizo sausage and shrimp on rice

Paian—a healer

Palaeolith—a stone tool dating to the Paleolithic period

Palanquin—a seat carried on poles on the shoulders used in ancient times to transport important people, especially in East Asia

Palazzo—a palatial building, especially in Italy

Paler—a slat of wood for a fence; a fenced-in area

Palfrey—a horse for everyday riding especially for a woman; a woman's riding horse

Palimpsest—a manuscript written over an older manuscript in such a way that the old words can be read

Palladium—a malleable silvery-white metallic element resembling platinum used in electrical contacts, jewelry and dental alloys

Palliasse—a thin straw mattress

Palliate—to reduce the intensity or severity of something; to attempt to make an offense less serious; to alleviate a symptom without curing the underlying condition

Palm—an oar blade; a unit of length based on the length or width of the hand

Palmetto—a low-growing palm plant with fan-shaped leaves; a blade of palmetto used for weaving

Palsie—refers to palsy or various types of paralysis accompanied by weakness, the loss of feeling and uncontrollable movements like shaking

Pampas—treeless grassy plains in temperate South America

Panace—a fabulous herb said by the ancients to be a panacea

Pancratiast—in ancient Greece a person skilled in the art of boxing or wrestling; a person skilled in boxing and wrestling

Pandanus—a palm-like plant with big roots and crown of narrow leaves

Pandar—a person who furthers illicit love affairs, a pimp or procurer, especially a male; to pander or assist in others' gratification

Pandit—a Hindu scholar learned in Sanskrit and Hindu philosophy and religion; a wise man or teacher; a talented musician

Panjandrum—a person who has or claims to have a great deal of authority or influence

Pannier—a basket on the back of an animal or other pack animal; a basket carried on a person's back; a cane framework worn by women on their hips in the eighteenth century to widen a skirt

Pannonia—a Roman province in present day Hungry and eastern Austria bounded on the north by the Danube River

Panopticon—an imaginary community created by Jeremy Bentham that consisted of a large courtyard with a tower at the center surrounded by a series of buildings divided into cells in which individuals are constantly visible, creating a supervising power that is constant and anonymous

Panorama—vie, scene, vista ; cf. diorama

Panthiest—the belief that God and the material world are one, God is present in everything and God is nature; the belief in the worship of all deities

Paphlagonia—an ancient area on the Black Sea coast north of central Anatolia between Bithynia and Pontus

Pappy—mushy, resembling pap

Pap—something like a book that lacks depth and substance and is thus considered trivial or worthless material

Par in parem non habet imperium—Latin for "equals have no sovereignty over each other," a general principle of international law establishing state immunity where one state cannot have jurisdiction over another sovereign state

Par ricochet—"indirectly" in French

Parabasis—in Old Greek comedy, when during intermission a chorus faces and addresses the audience directly

Paracelsus—a fifteenth-century Swiss physician who developed a new approach to medicine and philosophy based on observation and experience

Paraclete—in Christianity, the Holy Spirit

Paradisiacal—like or befitting a paradise

Parados—a bank built behind a trench that gives protection from attack from the rear

Paralogistic—in logic, an invalid argument that is unintentional or unnoticed

Paralytic—relating to paralysis; a person who is afflicted by paralysis

Paranoiac—relating to paranoia; somebody affected by paranoia

Paraphrase—to restate something using other words, especially to make it simpler or shorter; cf. metaphrase

Paraphrastic—paraphrase, restate something using other words, rephrase

Parcheggio—the act of parking a car; a car park area or building where cars park

Pardes Rimmonian—the title of an old Cabbalistic tract by Moses Cordovero representing the divine manifestation in which God emerges from his hidden state, they represent the female and male principles within the Godhead, espoused by Carl Jung

Parget—plaster, whitewash or any such material used to coat walls; ornamental plasterwork on walls

Pari passu—Latin for "with an equal step" or equal footing

Parisian—a person born and raised in Paris

Parochial—differences and relations within a single society; narrow, close-minded, insular or provincial; cf. catholic

Parsifal—an opera by Richard Wagner about Percival, an Arthurian knight, about his long quest for the Holy Grail

Parterre—an ornamental garden in a formal pattern with low evergreen hedges and annual bedding plants

Parti pris—a preconceived opinion or bias

Participle— a verb form that modifies another verb or noun, e.g. "working woman," "is going," "good breeding"

Particolor—having different colors in different areas or patches, variegated

Parti—the basic scheme or concept of an architectural design

Parva, si non fiant quotidie—Latin from Pliny for "small if it does not happen every day"

Passe-avants—cat walks on a boat

Pastiche—an artistic work in a style that imitates that of another work, artist or period

Pastilla—a Moroccan meat pie filled with spiced pigeon meat and apricots and having a sugared crust

Patavinity—linguistic provincialism

Patchily—occurring in patches; unpredictable and varying in quality, erratic, disconnected, unpredictable, variable

Patchouli—an aromatic oil from tropical mint used in perfumes

Paten—a shallow metal plate or dish typically made of gold or silver used for holding the bread during a religious ceremony

Pater Noster—the Lord's Prayer

Pate—the head, especially the top of the head

Pathetic fallacy—the attribution of human characteristics to nature, as in "an angry sea"

Pathos—a quality in human experience or art that evokes compassion; cf. bathos

Patrie—French for homeland

Patrimony—property inherited from one's father or male ancestor

Patristic—refers to early Christian writers like St. Augustine whose works helped shape the Christian Church

Patronal—relating to a patron saint

Patronymic—a name derived from a male ancestor, especially one with a suffix like "–son" as in Anderson

Patroon—an estate owner in New York or New Jersey during the Dutch colonial period

Pavid—to tremble, be afraid or timid

Pawkish humor—pawk means tricky or sly thus pawkish humor is scornful, mocking, cynical, sardonic or derisive

Pay—to cover with a composition that makes something watertight

Peccant—having committed a sin or fault, offending; diseased or causing disease

Pecuniary—relating to money; a financial penalty such as a fine

Pecunious—having plenty of money, moneyed, wealthy; cf. impecunious

Pedagogue—a teacher or educator; a pedantic or dogmatic teacher

Peepul—a large semi-evergreen tree with small figs, long stalks and broad leaves native to India in which Buddhists believe gods reside

Peerage—the title and rank of a peer; a class of people holding a hereditary honorary title

Pelagian—the belief that original sin did not influence human nature and that moral will is capable of choosing good and is possible without divine aid

Pelion and Ossa—adding difficulty to difficulty, fruitless efforts, the saying is from Greek mythology where the giants attempt to scale heaven by piling Mount Ossa upon Mount Pelion

Pellagra—a disease caused by dietary deficiency of niacin with symptoms of dermatitis, diarrhea and central nervous system disorders

Pellucid—allowing light to pass through, transparent; easy to understand or clear in meaning

Pelmeni—Russian dumplings with ground meat and onions

Peltast—in ancient Greece, light infantry

Pelt—to move quickly or extremely fast; a strong blow

Pemmican—a Native North American food made from strips of dried meat, pounded into a paste, mixed with fat and dried berries and pressed into small cakes, often used as an emergency ration

Penate—Roman gods who watch over the home or community

Pennant—a triangular flag displayed on boats for identification and signaling; in some sports, a flag that symbolizes a championship

Pennon—a long, narrow flag, usually triangular and tapering, carried on a lance by a medieval knight; same as a pennant

Pennyroyal—a reddish purple perennial herb used as an herbal remedy, in culinary dishes and as decoration

Pentad—any group or series of five; a period of five days in meteorology

Pentecontaetia—from historian Thucydides, the fifty-period in ancient Greek history between the defeat of the second Persian invasion in 479 BCE and the beginning of the Peloponnesian War in 433 BCE

Pentimenti—a technique of restoring paintings by removing the top layer of paint to reveal a painting underneath

Peparethus—a historian from the Greek island of Peparethus whose lost writings included histories of Persia and Rome

Peptonize—to digest food using an enzyme

Per contra—on the contrary, on the other hand, in contrast

Per fas aut nefas—Latin for "through right and wrong," which refers to unfair eristic treatment

Per fretum febris—"through the straits of fever" or by these straits I die

Perambulator—a baby carriage

Percale—a smooth, closely woven cotton or polyester fabric used for sheets and clothing

Peregrination—a journey or voyage

Perfidious Albion—an idiomatic expression for "treacherous England," "Faithless England" or "dirty, low-down, sneaky England"

Perfuse—to spread throughout something such as a liquid or color, to permeate something; to introduce a liquid into tissue by circulating it through blood vessels or other channels in the body, to inject a liquid into the body

Perian rose—a color halfway between red and magenta

Periauger—a shallow draft flat bottomed two-masted sailing vessel common in the late nineteenth and early twentieth centuries

Perihelion—the point of a planet, asteroid or comet at which it is closest to the sun; cf. aphelion

Perinatal—happening during or around the time of childbirth, especially from week twenty-eight of pregnancy to a month after birth

Perineum—the area between the anus and scrotum or vulva

Periochoresis—in religion, the relationship between each person of the Father, Son and Holy Spirit; from Greek, it means rotation

Perioecic—members of an autonomous and free group who were noncitizens in ancient Sparta

Peripeteia—a reversal of circumstances or turning point used primarily in literature

Peripety—an unexpected reversal or turn of events, especially in literature; a sudden change, as in fortune

Periphrasis—the use of long or indirect language, circumlocution; an expression that says something indirectly

Periphrastic—using two or more words rather than an inflected form, especially to describe a verb using an auxiliary verb, e.g. "did you have" is a periphrastic equivalent of "had you"

Peripities—a reversal of circumstances, or turning point, mostly in literature

Peristyle—a row of columns surrounding a space within a building such as a court or internal garden

Persicaria—a worldwide herbaceous flowering plant commonly known as knotweed or smartweed

Pertinacity—resolute in purpose, determined; cf. impertinent

Peruse—to read or examine something in a careful and through way; to read or scan something quickly

Pestle—a tool with a rounded end used for crushing and grinding substances; to crush or grind something with a pestle

Petit pas—small step in French; to be passionate about dance

Petitio principii—a circular argument that begs the question, the fallacious attempt to support a claim with a premise that presupposes the claim, e.g. "no greater being can be conceived, therefore God exists" assumes there is a being, God, who exists

Petits fours—a very small fancy cake, cookie or confection typically made with marzipan served after a meal; metaphorically, a reward for effort

Phaeton—a small light four-wheeled carriage usually with two seats drawn by two horses; an old-fashioned antique touring car

Phage—short for bacteriophage, which is a virus that infects and replicates within bacteria, derived from Greek meaning to devour

Phaleric bull—a bronze bull used to torture and execute people in ancient Greece by boiling them alive

Phanerogamica—a division of plants that have reproductive organs, a plant that produces seeds

Pharisaical—acting hypocritically, self-righteously and with obsessive regard to rules and formalities; relating to or characteristic of the Pharisees

Phial—a broad, shallow drinking vessel; a small vessel used to store medications, powders or capsules; same as vial, a small glass bottle especially for medicines

Philanopsis—a thick-leaved orchid with elegant blossoms

Philatelic—the collection and study of postage stamps and related items

Philautia—self-love, self-conceit, undue regard for oneself and one's own interests, considered a moral flaw

Philemon—to test people's piety, from Baucis in Phrygia who offered hospitality to Zeus and Hermes when they came to Earth without revealing their identities

Philhellene—an admirer of Greece, Greek history and culture

Philistia—in biblical times, the land of Philistia inhabited by Philistines

Philoctetes—in Greek mythology, a friend of Achilles and the slayer of the Trojan prince Paris

Philogostic—relating to inflammations and fevers; cf. phlogiston, dephlogistic

Philological—the study of the relationship between languages including their history based on texts; the study of ancient texts especially as they relate to the cultural history of a period of a people; the study of literature in general

Philology—the study of language in historical sources; the study of literary texts and written records

Philomela—in Greek mythology, frequently evoked as a symbol of literary, artistic and musical works, also known as the princess of Athens

Philopoemen—a skilled Greek general (253–183 BCE) and Achaean strategos

Philosophia ancilla theoloiae—Latin for "philosophy is the servant of theology" espoused by Thomas Aquinas

Philosophism—spurious or deceitful philosophy

Philtres—a potion, drug or charm supposed to be able to excite love; a potion to produce any magic effect

Phishing—an attempt to trick people into sharing sensitive information by inducing them to click on a bogus link or by pretending to be an entity

Phlebotomy—to make an incision in a vein in order to draw blood; a phlebotomist is one who draws blood

Phlegethon—in Greek mythology, one of the five rivers in the infernal regions of the underworld described as a stream of fire, it was said the goddess Styx was in love with Phlegethon, but she was consumed by his flames and sent to Hades

Phlegm—the thick mucus secreted in the respiratory system especially during a cold; calmness or composure, not easily disturbed, unflappable; in medieval medicine, one of the four bodily fluid humors thought to be cold and moist in nature and the cause of sluggishness and apathy

Phlogiston—a substance supposed by eighteenth-century chemists to exist in all combustible bodies and to be released by combustion; cf. Philogostic, dephlogistic

Phoebus—in Greek mythology the god Apollo when identified with the sun; a personification of the sun

Phoneme—the smallest speech sound or phonetic that distinguishes one word from another that carries the words meaning, e.g. the difference between immanent and imminent is one phoneme

Phrygian—somebody from ancient Phrygia

Phryne—a famous Greek courtesan who, because of her sallow complexion, was called a toad, a word that in Greek is phryne

Phylloxera—an aphid that is a major pest to wine-producing areas

Phylogenetic—relating to the evolutionary development and diversification of species or features of an organism

Phyrgians—people of Phrygia, an ancient nation in western Turkey

Physic—something that lifts the spirit or energizes; the profession of medicine; to treat someone with a cure; medicine, especially a purgative

Physiognomic—the features of a face, especially when indicators of a person's character; the judgment of character from facial features

Physiognomy—the features of a face, especially when they are used as indicators of character, temperament or ethnic origin

Physiologer—a physiologist, one who studies physiology

Pianoforte—same as piano

Piast—a Polish king who is of Polish ancestry and not foreign

Piazza—a covered passageway that has arches on one or both sides and is usually attached to a building

Pick-helve—a pickaxe without the head used as an unofficial baton

Pickwickian—generous, naïve or benevolent; not literal or typical in meaning

Picquet—another spelling of piquet or a card game for two with a deck that does not include two or six

Piebald—having irregular patches of two colors, typically black and white, as in a piebald horse,

Pied-à-terre—French meaning a foot on the ground meaning a secondary home, such as an apartment in town or room kept for occasional use

Pierglass—a large mirror used originally to fill wall space between windows

Pierogi—Polish dumplings with potatoes, sauerkraut, sour cream and egg dough

Pietistic—devotion to a deity and observance of religious principles, piousness; excessive or insincere religious devotion, sanctimoniousness

Piffle—to behave in a silly or ineffective way, to behave thoughtlessly; silly talk or ideas, nonsense

Pike-grey—a large, predatory freshwater fish with a long body, broad snout and sharp teeth native to northern waters

Pilaster—a vertical column of a building that projects partway from a wall and is made to resemble an ornamental column by adding a base and capital

Piles—hemorrhoids, painful varicose veins in the canal of the anus

Pillion—passenger seating, a side-seat, an extra seat

Pimento— also spelled pimiento, a large, sweet red pepper

Pinchbeck—an alloy of copper and zinc resembling gold used in watch making and costume jewelry; metaphorically, appearing valuable but actually cheap or tawdry

Pinion—the outer part of a bird's wing including the flight feathers; to hold down, trap, restrain, immobilize; cf. pinon

Pinnace—a small boat carried by a larger vessel used as a gig or tender

Pinner—a person or thing that pins; a small dainty apron; a cap with two long flaps pinned on

Pinon—a small pine tree with edible seeds, native to Mexico and the southwestern United States; cf. pinion

Pip—a small hard seed in a fruit; an excellent or very attractive person or thing; a mark or symbol on a playing card

Pipkin—a small metal or earthen cooking pot with a handle across the top

Pirogue—a flat-bottomed dug-out boat

Pirouette—in dance, the act of spinning on one foot, typically with the raised foot touching the knee of the supporting leg

Piscine—relating to or characteristic of fish

Piskie—a small faerie with wings

Pismire—archaic for an ant

Pistole—a French name given to a Spanish gold coin in use in the sixteenth century, the double escudo or gold unit

Pithiathism—an archaic medical term for hysteria that is curable by persuasive suggestion

Placable—capable of being placated, pacified or appeased; forgiving, tolerant; cf. implacable

Plaice—a large, flat-bodied ocean fish with brown skin and red spots native to European waters

Plaidoyer—an address, plea or argument made especially by a court advocate

Plainchant—in music, same as plainsong, church music that is intended to be sung in unison without instrumental accompaniment

Plainisphere—in astronomy, a star chart analog computing instrument in the form of two adjustable discs on a common pivot

Plaint—an expression of grief or sadness, plaintive or mournful, sad or melancholic; a complaint

Plaintive—expressing sadness or sounding sad

Plangent—a loud, reverberating and often melancholy sound

Plantagenet—a French royal house in Anjou which, for a period of time in the Middle Ages, held the English throne; relating to the English royal family that ruled between 1154 and 1485, or to this period of English history

Plash-splash; a sound produced by liquid striking something, to move through liquid scattering drops and light splashing sounds; a light splash or splashing sound

Pleasance— a secluded enclosure or part of a garden where the sole purpose is to give pleasure to the senses

Plebiscite—a direct vote by the entire electorate on an issue; a vote where a population exercises the right of national self-determination (a plebiscitory democracy is where the entire electorate votes)

Plectrum—a thin plastic or flexible material worn on the fingers used to pluck the strings of a musical instrument such as a guitar

Plenary—attended by every member or delegate; full or unlimited

Plenum—a full or general assembly, general attendance at a meeting; in philosophy, space entirely filled with matter

Pleonasm—the use of more words than are necessary to express a meaning, such as "free gift"

Pleroma—Greek for fullness or to fill up an empty thing; the totality of divine powers

Pleurisy—inflammation of the pleura surrounding the lungs that brings painful breathing, coughing and fluid buildup in the pleural cavity

Plication—the pleating and stitching of the walls of a body organ in order to reduce its size; the act of folding; a fold or pleat in something

Plighting—making a formal pledge such as in marriage

Plight—a formal pledge, especially in marriage

Plinth—a pedestal, platform, podium or dais; a square block beneath a column, pedestal or statue; a flat block used as a base for something, such as a heavy machine

Plover—a wading shorebird that has a short beak and tail and long, pointed wings

Plummet— a steep and rapid fall or drop

Pluperfect—even better than perfect; extreme in degree

Pneuma—the vital spirit, soul or creative force of a person

Pneumonic—plague that affects the lungs, symptoms include a bloody cough, high fever and difficulty breathing; cf. septicemic, bubonic

Pnyx—a hill in central Athens where Athenians assembled, thus making the hill an early important symbol of democracy

Poder moderador—a moderating power

Poetaster—a person who writes inferior poetry

Pogey bait—in Canada, unemployment or other welfare benefit

Poiesis—the making of things; cf. praxis

Poignard—a long, lightweight knife with a continuously tapering pointed blade

Poilu—a French infantry solider in World War One

Point d'appui—French for fulcrum, in military practice, the location where troops rally prior to a battle; a support or prop

Pointillé—a decorative technique similar to embossing in which patterns are formed on a surface by punching dots

Poleaxe—a pole ax, a butcher's ax with a hammer face opposite the blade used in slaughtering animals; a short battleax with a long or short handle with a hammer or spike opposite the blade

Polecat—a skunk

Polemology—the study of human aggressiveness

Polenta—a northern Italian dish of porridge or mush made from corn, farro, chestnuts and chickpeas

Pollard—to cut off the top branches of a tree to encourage new growth at the top

Pollux—in Greek and Roman mythology, Pollux is the twin of Castor, who had a different father; Pollux was the son of Zeus; in Roman mythology, Pollux asked Zeus to make him immortal so he could share it with his deceased brother Castor, which transformed them into the constellation Gemini; together they are regarded as the patrons of sailors and are associated with horsemanship

Polonaise—a woman's dress with a tight bodice and open skirt from the waist down looped to show a decorative underskirt; a vegetable dish garnished with egg yolk, bread and parsley

Polonius—a character in Shakespeare's *Hamlet* whose character depicts a busybody, officious, garrulous and impertinent, blowhard, tedious old fool who consistently makes wrongful judgments

Poltergeist—a supernatural being like a ghost that is supposedly responsible for physical disturbances

Polyandry—the custom of having more than one husband at the same time; cf. exogamy, endogamy, polygamy, monogamy

Polycarp—a second-century Christian bishop who combated Christian heresy; a martyr for the truth

Polydaemonism—the belief in a multitude of demons or spiritual powers

Polygamy—the custom of having more than one spouse at the same time; cf. exogamy, endogamy, polyandry, monogamy

Polyptyque—archaic for an inventory

Polypus—a small stalk-shaped growth sticking out from the skin that is usually benign but sometimes malignant

Pomade—a perfumed oil or ointment used to make the hair look smooth and shiny, a dressing for hair

Pomander—an aromatic mixture of substances enclosed in a container to impart a pleasant smell

Pomerania—a historical region of north-central Europe bordering on the Baltic Sea in present-day northwest Poland and northeast Germany

Pommel—the end of the hilt or handle on a sword

Pomology—the study of cultivating fruit

Pompon—a small woolen ball attached to a garment for decoration, especially a hat

Pomum—Latin for apple

Pone—same as the food cornpone (cf. cornpone for an alternate definition), fried or baked bread made with cornmeal

Popish—an offensive term meaning associated with the Roman Catholic Church, its doctrines and practices

Poplicola—Publius Valerius Poplicola or Publicola was an aristocratic ancient Roman who helped overthrow the monarchy, which ushered in the Roman Republic; the authors of the *Federalist Papers* referred to him as Publius in his honor

Pore—to study something carefully and thoughtfully

Porphyria—a group of disorders caused by abnormalities in the chemical steps that lead to heme production that usually cause nerve and skin problems

Porphyry—a reddish purple rock containing feldspar crystals; any fine grained igneous rock that contains large crystals; Greek Neo-Platonic philosopher circa 234–305 BCE know for opposing Christianity

Portcullis—a heavy iron or wooden grating set in grooves that lower to block access to a castle

Portia—a small inner moon of Uranus; heroine in Shakespeare's *Merchant of Venice*

Portion—to give a dowry to a woman; an unavoidable event or part of somebody's life, fate

Poser—a difficult question or problem

Positum—something that is posited or laid down, to suggest something, especially to start a discussion

Possessio—the act of taking, holding, occupying or possessing property

Post chaise—a horse-drawn carriage with four wheels used in the eighteenth and nineteenth centuries

Post festum—Latin for "after the feast" and figuratively too late or after the fact

Post hoc ergo propter hoc—Latin for "after this therefore because of this," known as the logical fallacy that assumes one event is caused by a previous event, e.g. the rooster crows, the sun rises, therefore the rooster causes the sun to rise

Post-horse—a horse used by couriers or mail carriers

Postilion—somebody riding on the left front horse in a team of horses drawing a carriage

Postprandial—occurring after a meal, especially an evening meal

Potesse—to be able, can; cf. esse

Pother—a state of emotional agitation, especially over something trivial; a great deal of frenzied activity over something trivial; a suffocating cloud of smoke or dust

Potsherd—a fragment or piece of broken pottery, especially one found at an archeological site; a piece of earthenware

Pouffe—a puffed-out hairstyle similar to a bouffant fashionable in the eighteenth century

Poultice—a soft, moist plant material applied to the body to reduce pain and inflammation, a warm, moist preparation placed on an inflamed part of the body to ease pain, improve circulation or hasten pus, a moist substance applied to an injury; cf. fomentation

Praecox—pertaining to something that occurred at an earlier stage of life or development; dementia praecox includes several psychotic disorders characterized by distortions of reality and disturbances of thought and withdrawal from social contact

Pragnänz—from Gestalt psychology, the idea that sensory input is organized based on certain rules

Pram—a buggy or pushchair

Pratten—to act

Prau—same as proa, a Malayan sailboat with a triangular sail

Pravity—archiac for wickedness, badness, foulness and physical corruption, moral degeneracy, perversion, corruption, poor quality or unwholesomeness; cf. depravity

Praxis—action, to act; cf. poiesis

Praxitelean—relating to the ancient Greek fourth-century sculptor Praxiteles

Prebend—an allowance paid by a church to a member of its clergy

Prebendary—a member of the clergy of a cathedral or collegiate church

Precentor—a person who leads a congregation in singing or prayers

Precept—a general rule intended to regulate behavior or thought; a writ or warrant

Preceptor—a teacher responsible to uphold a certain law, tradition or precept

Prefect—a high-ranking administrative official; in ancient Rome, a senior administrative or military official

Prefecture—the office, jurisdiction or territory of a church prefect; cf. prefect

Prelate—a high-ranking member of the Christian clergy such as an abbot, bishop or cardinal

Premier cru—the first in importance, the best or most important; a prime minister or head of government

Premoral—time before the development of morality; not having an understanding of right and wrong

Presbytery—the home of a Roman Catholic parish priest

Presentiment—an awareness of some future event, especially an unpleasant one before it happens, a feeling that something will happen

Prester—a waterspout or whirlwind

Pretera censeo—Latin for "and furthermore I think" made famous by the Roman Cato who would end his speeches with "et preterea censeo Carthago delenda est" or "and furthermore, I think Carthage must be destroyed"

Preterite—a verb tense expressing something that happened in the past (in the sentence "I felt angry with them" the verb felt is in the preterite tense)

Pretermission—to overlook or ignore something intentionally, especially a natural heir in a will; to leave something out or undone

Preternatural—Latin for beyond natural, that which appears outside or beside what is natural, exceptional or abnormal; cf. supernatural

Preux—chivalrous, gallant

Prim—a person easily shocked by vulgar or obscene behavior, prudish; excessively neat and tidy; excessively formal and proper in manner and appearance

Prime—the first hour of daylight, sunrise or about six a.m.; cf. Matins, Lauds, Vespers, Compline

Primus inter pares—Latin for first among equals usually attributed to one who is formally equal but accorded unofficial respect

Prince Albert coat—a knee length man's coat popular during the Victorian period

Principal—first in order of importance; main; the person with the highest authority; cf. principle

Principle—an important law or assumption required in a system of thought; the basic way something works; the primary source of something; cf. principal

Prink—to dress or groom somebody or yourself in a fancy or fussy way

Prior—an officer in a monastery of rank below an abbot; a man who is superior in some religious communities

Prioress—a woman officer in a convent at a rank below abbess; a woman superior in some religious communities

Priory—a monastery or convent

Prius—something preceding, especially a necessary prior condition, from Latin meaning something preceding

Privatio boni—in theology, the doctrine that evil is insubstantial so thinking of it as an entity is misleading, rather evil is the absence of good

Probative—designed to test or prove something, to test; providing proof or evidence

Probe—a dash used at the beginning and end of a comment that interrupts the flow of a sentence

Procaine—a white, colorless crystalline ester used as an anesthetic; cf. ester

Proceleusmatic—inciting, animating, encouraging; in poetry or music, consisting of a metrical foot of four short syllables used in the latter case in ancient times to animate rowers of galleys

Prodos—a side entrance in an ancient Greek theater; the first song sung by the chorus in ancient Greek theater after its entrance from the prodos; cf. stasima

Prodrome—a symptom indicating the onset of a disease, a fore-warning symptom

Profane—showing disrespect for God or religion, irreverent; to treat something irreverently; not connected with religious matters, secular

Proffer—to hold something out to somebody so that they can grasp it; to offer something for consideration, a proposal

Prolapse—a slippage or sinking of a body organ or part; to be displaced in the body

Prolate—in a sphere, lengthened in the direction of the polar diameter

Prolusion—a preliminary exercise, a trial before the principle performance, a prelude

Prone—lying horizontally with the face or torso faced down; cf. supinity

Prong—a branch of a river

Pronominal—like or functioning as a pronoun

Pronunciamento—a political manifesto or proclamation

Propaedeutic—serving as preliminary instruction to further study; an introduction to a subject or area of study

Prophanation—obsolete for profanation or profanity, the use of course or offensive language, the use of foul or vulgar words; contempt for God or sacred principles; irreligious

Propinquity—nearness in space, time or relationship

Propria—in logic, properties that are not part of an essence but follow from it so they are universal to the species, e.g. capable of laughter, in the case of mankind

Propter amorem—Latin for "all for love"

Propylaea—a colonnaded gate or entrance to a building, especially to a temple

Prorogation—to discontinue parliamentary procedure without formally ending the session, to suspend a parliamentary session; to postpone something to a later date

Prorogue—to discontinue a parliamentary system informally; to postpone or defer something to a later date

Proscenium—that part of a theater stage in front of the curtain; the stage of an ancient theater

Prosodist—one who studies the structure of poetry and the techniques in writing it

Prosody—the study of the structure of poetry and its conventions and techniques; a system or theory of writing poetry; the rhythm of speech including stress and intonation

Prosopopeia—a figure of speech that presents an imaginary dead or absent person speaking; a figure of speech where human qualities are attributed to objects or abstract notions

Prospice—Latin for examine the future; cf. respice, adspice

Protagonist—the first actor in ancient Greek plays; cf. deuterogonist, tritagonist

Protention—duration; the process of stretching forth

Proto—first in time, earliest; original, ancestral

Protonotary—a chief clerk in some courts of law, originally in Byzantine courts

Proursuivant—a pursuer, a chaser; a persecutor or tormenter

Provender—food for livestock, especially hay or fodder; food

Pruritus—to itch, the unpleasant sensation that causes the desire to scratch

Psalmodies—the singing of psalms in divine worship; a collection of psalms

Psalter—a book containing psalms used in worship

Pseudepiscopy—the existence of a spurious or pretended bishop

Pseudocyesis—a false pregnancy

Psychagogue—a noun, or that type of word the meaning of which determines reality and provides names for all things

Psychasthenic—in psychiatry, a neurosis marked by fear, anxiety and phobias as well as extreme indecisiveness, timidity and a tendency toward fixed ideas

Psychographics—the study and classification of people according to their attitudes, aspirations, and other psychological criteria, often used in market analysis

Psychoid—soul-like or quasi-psychic

Psychomachy—the conflict of the soul between the spirit and the flesh, the internalized battle between spirit and flesh

Psychotomimetic—a mimicker of madness

Pudenda—the human body's external genital organs

Puer—a variety of fermented tea; Latin for "eternal boy," in mythology the child-god who is forever young; in psychology, an older person whose emotional life has remained at an adolescent level

Puissance—strength, power or might; the power to persuade or influence people; the ability to exert effort to accomplish a task

Pukka—genuine or authentic; of the highest quality or standard; well done or well made; of high social status, respectable

Pulping—making a soft or soggy mass; making cheap novels or magazines especially on crime, horror or science fiction

Pulque—a thick Mexican alcoholic drink made from the sap of the agave plant

Pulse—a plant with pods as fruit such as pea, bean or alfalfa; an edible seed from a pod

Punctilio—strict adherence to the finest points of etiquette

Punt—a long narrow flat-bottomed boat square at both ends propelled by long poles and used on inland waterways

Purblind—having impaired or defective vision; slow or unable to understand, dimwitted

Purdah—the Hindu and Islamic custom of keeping women fully covered with clothing and apart from society, keeping women from public view; a screen or curtain used in some Hindu communities to keep women out of view; a veil worn by Muslim and Hindu women as part of purdah

Purism—the effort to purify a language such as French or Italian; cf. cruscantism

Purled—knitted with a purl stitch

Purlieu—the outer regions or boundaries of a place, the environs; a district on the outskirts of a city; a frequented place; in the United Kingdom, an area or district that is old and poor

Purloin—to take something, to steal, filch or pilfer

Purulence—pus

Purulent—relating to or consisting of pus; cf. septic, suppurate

Purusa—the Hindu primeval being

Purveyance—in the medieval ages, the king's right when traveling to commandeer supplies for a number of miles on either side of the road; to provision an army

Pusillanimous—a contemptible lack of boldness, weak-spirited, cowardly

Puttee—a leather or cloth covering of the lower leg from the knee the ankle, especially worn as part of a military uniform

Putto—in the Baroque period, an infant boy or cherub, often with wings

Pyemia—a disease caused by pus-forming microorganisms in the bloodstream, blood poisoning

Pyrite—an iron sulfide mineral with a brassy metallic luster that is a source of iron and sulfur

Q

Quadran—a low-value Roman bronze coin

Quadrate—a square or cube area, space or thing; in some animals, a bony cartilaginous part of the upper jaw that articulates with the lower jaw at the sides of the skull

Quadrille—a dance fashionable in the late eighteenth and nineteenth centuries in Europe and its colonies performed by four couples in a rectangular formation, similar to American square dancing

Quaesitum—Latin for something sought for, an end or objective; the sought solution to a problem

Quais—the area of a city alongside water like a harbor

Quaker gun—a wooden log painted black to resemble a real gun used to deceive the enemy in eighteenth- and nineteenth-century warfare

Quant—a complex thinking person who deals in concepts beyond the grasp of most linear imaginations and who speaks a language that is understood only by other quants

Quartan—a mild form of malaria causing a fever that recurs every third day

Quatrain—a verse of poetry consisting of four lines with alternate lines often rhyming

Quay—a concrete, stone or metal platform lying alongside water for loading and unloading ships

Qucklime—calcium oxide, commonly known as quicklime or burnt lime, a white, caustic, alkaline, crystalline solid

Quern—a stone mill used for grinding grain by hand

Querulant—having a quarrelsome, argumentative and suspicious nature

Quested—a search or pursuit made in order to find or obtain something

Quetzal—a bird with brilliant green and red feathers and a long streaming tail native to Central and South America; the main unit of currency in Guatemala

Queue—a short braid of hair at the back of the head worn by nineteenth sailors

Qui vive—to be on the lookout or alert

Quibble—a pun, a play on words

Quiberon peninsula—a peninsula in Brittany in western France

Quibuscumque viis—to succeed by any means, in any way

Quicksilver—tending to change rapidly and unpredictably; same as mercury

Quiddity—the essence or real nature of something; an unimportant or trifling distinction

Quill—in textiles, a spindle or bobbin onto which yarn is wound

Quince—an aromatic pear-shaped yellow fruit that comes from the quince tree

Quincunx—an arrangement of five objects in a square, with four at the corners and one in the center

Quinsie—pus due to an infection behind the tonsil that causes fever, throat pain and trouble opening the mouth

Quintain—a target used by medieval knights for jousting practice

Quintal—in the metric system, a unit of weight equal to 100 kg, same as hundredweight

Quipu—a rope depicting an ancient Incan language with knots and different colors

Quire—in printing, a collection of twenty-four or twenty-five sheets of paper, one twelfth of a ream

Quitrent—in feudal times, rent paid by a tenant to a landlord in exchange for a release from some feudal obligations

Quitted—departed from a place

Quod non—Latin meaning they condemn what they do not understand

Quod—in the United Kingdom, the same as jail

Quoits—a game where players throw rings over a small post

Quotron—a computer system or service that provides stock market quotations

R

Rabe—broccoli rabe is a green cruciferous vegetable

Radiolarian—a protozoa with a minimal skeleton found in the ocean

Raft—a dense flock of swimming birds or mammals

Raga—traditional South Asian music associated with different times of the day and intended to create different moods

Ragout—a rich, slow-cooking stew of meat and vegetables; a stew

Rakehell—a dissolute, licentious man, a rake; profligate

Rameau—Jean-Philippe Rameau was an important French music composer and theorist of the eighteenth century; cf. Lilli

Ranker—a private in the army; an officer who previously was a private

Rankly—to grow profusely with excessive vigor; highly fertile such as rank land that yields excessive crops

Rapporteur—a person appointed to report on an organization's meetings

Rapt—completely fascinated by what one is seeing or hearing

Rastafarian—a monolithic religion rooted in Christianity with a single god and a social movement developed in Jamaica in the 1930s

Ratafia—a sweet fruit liqueur

Raté—to miss, misfire, fail, bungle

Rattan—long, thin, jointed stems used in wickerwork, furniture and canes; furniture made of rattan

Réamur scale—a French temperature scale where freezing is 0 degrees and boiling is 80 degrees

Rebus principle—the representation of a word by a picture of an object the name of which resembles in sound the word

Recitative—a musical declamation in opera sung in the rhythm of ordinary speech with many words on the same note, e.g. singing in recitative; cf. declamation

Rectilinear—involving a straight line

Recurril—Spanish meaning to turn to, to resort to; to recur

Recur—to have recourse

Redingote—a woman's coat with an open, full skirt and close-fitting top; a man's double-breasted overcoat with wide flat cuffs popular in the eighteenth century

Redintegration—in philosophy, restoration to a unified state, literally the "part reinstates the whole"

Reductionism—the practice of analyzing complex phenomena at a simpler or more fundamental level, especially when it ostensibly results in a sufficient explanation

Reductive fallacy—an invalid deductive argument in which the argument may have a true premises but a false conclusion, e.g. all birds have beaks; that creature has a beak, therefore that creature is a bird is a fallacy because octopuses also have beaks

Re-entrant—the low ground formed between two hill spurs; an enemy's line facing a salient in military tactics; cf. salient

Reforma—Spanish meaning reform; cf. ruptura

Refrain—something that is frequently repeated such as a saying, an idea or a part of a song in music

Reft—past for reave, to carry out raids in order to plunder; to rob someone by force; to steal something

Regnant—reigning, ruling; currently having the greatest influence, dominant

Reins—the lower region of the trunk including the kidneys, lower abdomen, hips and lower back

Reiterate—to say or do something several times, often in a tiresome way; cf. iterate

Relatum—a thing or term related; one of a group of related things

Relict—in biology, a species surviving long after the extinction of a related species or a species surviving only in isolation; to survive unchanged; in law, a woman whose husband has died or a woman whose partner regularly goes away

Relievo—same as relief, to relieve from tension or anxiety

Reliquary—a container or shrine for relics such as the remains of saints

Remanence—the magnetic nature that remains in a substance after the magnetizing field has been removed; figuratively, the residual or that which remains

Remedial—acting as a remedy or solution to a problem; in medicine, something intended to cure or relieve illness; education designed to help people with learning difficulties

Remonstrance—a forceful argument in favor or against something; a formal protest, usually in the form of a document or petition

Renascent—showing new life or activity, newly active

Rennet—the inner lining of the stomach of calves; a substance made from rennet used in making cheese

Repletion—the condition of being overly full due to eating too much; the condition of being fully satisfied

Replevin—in law, an act to recover goods from someone who claims to own them and who promises to have the claim later tested in court

Repost—to end something like a letter for a second or further time; to post something online for a second or further time; a message, link or image that has been reposted

Repustrian—composed of rocks, inscribed on rock

Requite—to return a kindness or hurt someone has done, to pay something back; to pay back for a service performed, cf. unrequite

Reredo—an altarpiece or screen behind an altar in a church, usually depicting religious images

Res cogitans—Latin meaning a thinking thing; cf. res extensa

Res extensa—Latin meaning an extended thing or substance, a material substance; cf. res cogitans

Res gestae—in law, the events that relate to a particular case, especially as admissible evidence

Rescript—an official edict or announcement

Resect—to surgically remove part of something

Resinier—French meaning to reconcile oneself to, to yield; to give up a right to, to yield

Resipiscence—a change of mind or heart, often to return to a sane, sound or correct view or position; a reformation

Respice—Latin meaning examine the past; cf. adspice, prospice

Respire—to breathe; to recover hope, courage or strength after a time of difficulty

Retainer—a servant or follower of a noble or wealthy person, especially one that has worked for them for a long time

Reticule—a small fabric purse carried by women in the late eighteenth and early nineteenth centuries

Retransmission—the process of transmitting; the transference of force between machines

Retrocession—to go back or return; to give something like territory back to somebody

Retrograde—moving backward in space or time; worsening or returning to an earlier worse condition; in writing, inverse or reversed in order

Revanchist—a nation's policy of regaining lost territory

Reverie—a state of idle and pleasant contemplation, a daydream

Revertant—to revert to a normal phenotype, usually by mutation; a spontaneous correction of a pathogenic mutation in a somatic cell

Revetment—a facing added to a structure that provides additional support; a barricade constructed to prevent damage or injury from explosives

Riband—a ribbon, especially one used for decorative purposes

Ribbly—having prominent ribs, a ribby fabric

Ricotta—a soft, white, mild-tasting Italian cheese made from whey

Rictus—a fixed open-mouthed grin or grimace, especially as an expression of horror; the gape of a bird's beak

Ridden—harassed, oppressed, or obsessed by, usually due to guilt; excessively full of or supplied with

Rifled—a gun or cannon with spiral grooves in the bore that give greater accuracy over a long distance

Rill—a small stream; a small channel cut in soil

Rime—an old spelling for rhyme

Rinderpest—a viral disease affecting cattle, sheep and goats marked by fever, hemorrhage and diarrhea found mostly in central Africa and Asia

Rind—the tough outer layer of a fruit; a tough outer layer; figuratively. to have an outer-skin-like shape

Riposte—a quick, witty response to someone; in fencing, a quick deft thrust made after parrying the lunge of an opponent

Riverine—resembling a river; located or living beside a river, e.g. a riverine people

Rive—to split or tear apart violently

Roan—having a reddish-brown, brown or black coat speckled with white or gray hairs

Rock alum—an eighteenth-century colorless writing fluid that becomes visible with water

Rockbound—hemmed in, enclosed or covered by rocks

Rodomontade—boastful or inflated talk or behavior

Roebuck—a male roe dear, especially an adult one

Rogation—days of prayers and fasting in Western Christianity

Roma—the Italian name for Rome

Roman à clef—a novel in which characters are based on real people whose identities are disguised that includes clues to their true characters and identities

Romance of the rose—poetry about women and in particular medieval clerks writing against women

Rondeaux—a poem in three stanzas where the opening phrase is repeated twice as an unrhymed refrain; a medieval French song, especially a trouvère song with a two-part refrain

Rondo—a piece of instrumental music in which a theme is repeated in contrast with the last movement

Rook—a large bird of the crow family that nests in colonies in tree tops; a swindler or cheat, especially at cards

Rosicrucian—a seventeenth-century spiritual and cultural movement built on esoteric truths of the ancient past about nature, the universe and the spirit realm concealed from the average man

Rosin—a hard translucent resin often used between the bow and strings of some stringed instruments; a hard resin

Rota—the supreme ecclesiastical tribunal of the Catholic Church; a list of people's names in the order in which they carry out duties

Rotifer—a microscopic invertebrate with a wheel-shaped crown of cilia at the anterior that lives mostly in freshwater

Rotogravure—a printing process in which images are etched onto copper cylinders and then put on a rotary press and printed on moving paper

Roturier—a common man, plebeian, populare, prolétaire

Roulade—food on a plate coated with sauce rolled and cooked so to give a spiral appearance; several musical notes sung rapidly to one syllable

Rubicund—a reddish skin color regarded as a sign of good health, rosy

Rudolphine tables—a star catalogue and planetary tables published by Johannes Kepler in 1627

Ruff—a separate collar of starched pleated linen or lace worn in the sixteenth and seventeenth centuries; long colorful hair or feathers on the neck of a bird or other animal

Ruminant—any cud-chewing hoofed mammal with an even number of toes and stomach with multiple chambers; inclined to be thoughtful and reflective

Runic—a mysterious symbol imbued with magical power; a character in an ancient Germanic runic alphabet

Runlet—a small river or stream

Ruptura—Spanish meaning to break; breaking, breech; cf. reforma

Ryot—in Asia, a subsistence farmer with a small piece of land

S

Sabot—a wooden shoe formerly worn in France; a strap across the instep of a sandal

Sabretache—a small leather case worn on a cavalryman's belt

Sachem—a chief of a native North American people; in political history a leader of Tammany Hall

Sackcloth—a course cloth made from goat hair used to make sacks; clothes made from sackcloth worn as a sign of mourning or penitence

Sacristan—an officer of the church in charge of the sacristy, church contents and their contents in ancient times; cf. sacristy

Sacristy—a room in a church keeping vestments and other church furnishings, sacred vessels and parish records; cf. sacristan

Saddhus—in Hinduism sadhu or a Hindu holy man who lives by begging

Sadic—a sadist, one who gains pleasure from others' pain or discomfort

Sado—in Malaysian slang, one who is strong and muscular; slang for sadomasochism, to enjoy inflicting pain or suffering on another

Saffron—an orange colored stigma ground to powder used as a food colorant or for flavoring

Sahel—the climatic zone of transition between the Sahara Desert and the Sudanese Savanna in Africa

Sahib—an Indian form of respectful address to men, formerly used to address white men during the colonial period

Sais—a stableman or groom; an ancient Egyptian provincial capital town in the western Nile Delta

Salente—in Irish, a salutation or toast, often to good health

Salient—a battlefield feature that projects into enemy territory that is surrounded by the enemy on three sides, making them vulnerable; cf. re-entrant

Sallow—unnaturally pale or yellowish; yellowish skin indicative of poor health

Salto mortale—From Italian, salto means "leap" and mortale means "deadly," hence a fateful or dangerous decision

Salver—a typically silver tray used in formal occasions

Salvianus—a fifth-century French writer on antiquity and particularly ancient Rome

Samarkand—one of the oldest cities of Central Asia, the most famous city of modern Uzbekistan and the object of the novel *The Road to Samarcand* by Patrick O'Brian

Samh—a wild flower

Samovar—a large, often-ornate Russian tea urn

Samskara—a Hindu purification ceremony that marks a transition in a person's life, a rite of passage; the idea that all our thoughts, words, feelings, actions and behaviors in life create impressions on our consciousness that act like scars

Sanctus—a hymn in Christianity praising the power and holiness of God; a musical setting for the Sanctus

Sandfly fever—a mild viral disease characterized by fever, malaise, eye pain and headache transmitted by sandflies occurring usually in warmer parts of the world, also known as pappataci, phlebotomus and three-day fever

Sangar—a small low breastwork built around an existing hollow in the ground

Sansculottisme—relating to the revolutionary poorer classes sans-culottes during the French Revolution who had contempt for the aristocracy

Sap—a covered trench dug to get inside enemy territory; a tunnel built under fortifications in order to weaken them

Saphead—slang for a foolish or gullible person, a simpleton, idiot or fool

Sapientia cordis—wisdom of the heart

Sapper—a military engineer who specializes in tunnels dug under enemy territory; a military engineer who lays, detects and disarms mines

Sapsucker—an American woodpecker that pecks rows of small holes in trees for sap and insects

Saraband—a dignified seventeenth- and eighteenth-century Spanish court dance

Saracen—Muslims who fought against the Christian Crusaders in the Middle Ages; a member of ancient desert people in Syria and Arabia; same as Arab

Sarc—same as sacro, striated muscle, flesh

Sardonic—scornful, mocking, sarcastic, derisive, cutting criticism

Sardonyx—a semiprecious stone that is a variety of onyx with orange, brown and white chalcedony bands

Sashweight—a counterweight to a vertically sliding window sash

Satori—in Buddhism, a state of objective spiritual enlightenment

Satyagraha—political passive resistance and non-cooperation, the political philosophy of Gandhi

Satyriasis—uncontrollable or excessive sexual desire in a man; cf. nymphomania

Sawyer—a horned beetle whose larvae bore into trees

Sbirri—slang in Italian for police, plural of sbirro

Sbirro—in Italy, a policeman; a ruffian or henchman

Scalene—a triangle in which each side is a different length, a triangle that lacks two equal sides

Scalenum—describing a scalene triangle, each side of which is a different length

Scallion—a long-necked, usually green onion with a small bulb

Scamp—to do something hastily, carelessly or in a perfunctory manner

Scansion—the analysis of verse according to the rules of meter; the way verse or a poem scans, a poem's metrical structure

Scapegrace—a lazy, mischievous or irresponsible person, especially a child

Scarab—a large dung beetle of the eastern Mediterranean area, regarded as sacred in Egypt; an ancient gem in the form of a scarab beetle, sometimes depicted with the wings spread, engraved in hieroglyphs

Scarcenesse—obsolete for scarce, restricted in quantity

Scarlatina—same as scarlet fever

Scarper—to run away

Sceptic—another spelling of skeptic

Schadenfreude—malicious or smug pleasure taken in another's misfortune, gloating at another's bad luck

Schismatic—relating to schism; a promoter in the cause of a schism

Schist—a rock whose minerals have aligned themselves in one direction that is thus capable of being split in parallel layers

Schnorrer—a beggar or scrounger, a layabout

Scholium—a medieval annotation or commentary written on an ancient Greek or Latin text

Sciatica—pain from the hip down to the calf usually caused by a protruding disc pressing on the sciatic nerve

Scimitar—a curved Arab sword that broadens as it nears the point

Scipionic circle—a group of scholars and philosophers that gathered at the home of Roman Scipio Aemilianus; a group of scholars and philosophers

Scirrhus—a carcinoma that is hard to the touch

Scission—the act of cutting, separating or dividing

Scone—a small baked bread served split and buttered; British plain scones that are served with jam and cream with tea

Scoop—to hit a ball upward from beneath so that it rises

Scopare—to have sexual intercourse

Scotomize—to avoid or deny something undesirable through the creation of a mental "blind spot"

Scrim—a curtain in theater that appears opaque to the audience and transparent from behind

Scritoire—a variant of escritoire, a secretary's desk made with wide drawers, a hinged desktop and topped by a bookcase

Scrofula—tuberculosis of the lymph glands, especially in the neck, that results in running sores on the skin; cf. scrofulous

Scrofulous—morally corrupt and degenerate; rundown, shabby or diseased in appearance; characteristic of scrofula; cf. scrofula

Scudded—to run or move quickly or hurriedly; in nautical terms, to run before a gale with little or no sail; in archery, an arrow that flies too high and wide of the mark

Scud—to move fast in a straight line because or as if driven by the wind; a formation of clouds driven fast by the wind

Scullery—a small kitchen or room at the back of a house used for washing dishes and other dirty household work

Scullion—a servant who does menial kitchen chores

Scuole—the Scuole Grandi was a fraternity institution in Venice, Italy founded in the thirteenth century as a charitable and religious institution that was involved in the development of music

Scurrility—coarseness, vulgarity or lack of refinement; language that is coarse and vulgar

Scurrilous—insulting, scandalous, slanderous or outrageous behavior

Scurvy—a disease caused by insufficient vitamin C, the symptoms of which include spongy gums, loosening of the teeth and bleeding from the skin and mucous membranes

Scutcheon—archaic spelling of escutcheon; cf. escutcheon

Scuttle—a bucket-like container for coal

Scylla—in ancient Greek mythology, a female sea monster who devoured sailors when they tried to navigate the narrow channel between her cave and the whirlpool Charybdis; in later legend, a dangerous rock located on the Italian side of the Strait of Messina

Sea mew—any of the various sea gulls

Sear—to have a sudden painful or unpleasant effect; a catch that holds a gunlock cocked

Secesh—a secessionist, a supporter of the Confederacy during the United States Civil War

Secretary—a writing desk with shelves on top of it

Sectary—a member of a religious or political sect

Seducible—lead astray, for example, from duty or rectitude; persuaded to have sexual intercourse

Seethe—to boil, or churn or foam as if boiling

Seigneurial—similar to manorialism; in French, feudal society manor with a lord called the seigneur

Seignorage—a duty tax

Seines—a large fishing net with weights to hang vertically in water

Selvage—an edge of fabric that is woven so that it will not fray; a strip of material that allows something to be handled; the decorative fringe on the ends of an Oriental rug

Semantic—relating to the meaning or differences between meanings of words or symbols; in logic, relating to the conditions in which a system or theory can be true

Semaphore—a system of signaling using hand held flags that are moved to represent alphabetical letters; a signaling device for sending information using mechanical arms mounted on a post, especially on a railroad

Semiotic—the study of meaning-making, in philosophy, the theory of signs and symbols that deals with their function

Semi-sepoy—a native solider, often Indian, usually an infantry-man in service of Europeans, especially the British

Semite—a member of a Semitic-speaking people of including the Arab and Jewish peoples as well as the ancient Assyrians, Babylonians, Carthaginians, Ethiopians and Phoenicians; an offensive term for a Jew

Semolina—the hard grains left after the milling of flour used in puddings and pasta

Sempach—a medieval sword with a very stiff blade of hexagonal section

Sempiternal—eternal, everlasting and unchanging

Sempstress—same as seamstress

Seneschal—in medieval times, a steward who managed the domestic staff of a noble house

Senna—a leguminous plant with yellow flowers in clusters found in temperate regions used as a purgative or laxative

Sentence—a group of words that express a complete thought, feeling or idea; in law, a judgment by a court specifying punishment for a crime

Sentiment écoeurant—something that gives a sickening, disgusted or horrified feeling or makes you feel sick to your stomach

Sepia—a deep reddish-brown pigment used in painting; a drawing with brownish tone; dark brown

Sepoy—in British India, an Indian solider under British command

Seppuku—Japanese ritualistic suicide involving disembowelment with a sword, same as hara-kiri

Septem Sermones—a collection of mystical Gnostic texts privately published by Carl Jung in 1916 under the title *Seven Sermons to the Dead*

Septennial—lasting seven years; occurring every seven years

Septicemia—blood poisoning, especially caused by bacteria

Septicemic—describing the type of plague where plague bacteria multiply in the bloodstream; patients develop fever, chills, weakness and abdominal pain; cf. bubonic, pneumonic

Septic—infected with bacteria, festering, suppurating, puss-filled, putrid, like something poisoned, diseased or purulent; cf. suppurate, purulent

Septuagint—a Greek version of the Jewish Scriptures redacted in the third and second centuries BCE by Jewish scholars and adopted by Greek-speaking Christians

Sepulchral—relating to burial vaults or funerals and burials; possessing characteristics associated with the grave; figuratively dismal, gloomy

Sequin—a gold coin that was used in Venice and Turkey between the sixteenth and eighteenth centuries

Serac—a ridge, pinnacle or block of ice in a crevasse or slope of a glacier

Seraglio—the same as harem, the woman's part of the house in traditional Muslim society reserved for wives and concubines; a Turkish palace, especially the Ottoman sultan's palace at Istanbul

Sere—dry or withered

Serge—a strong cloth usually made of wool used to make coats, jackets and pants; e.g. a serge suit

Seriatim—one after another, or in a series

Serried—crowded together with little space between each, close together

Servanda—things to be maintained or saved; cf. delenda

Servator mundi—Latin for "savoir of the world"

Servitor—a person who attends or serves a social superior

Seton—in medicine a thread, gauze, wire or other material passed through the subcutaneous tissues to form a sinus

Settle—in veterinary medicine, to make an animal pregnant, or to become pregnant

Severetus—Michael Severetus was a sixteenth-century Renaissance man, writer and professor who did not accept religious orthodoxy or the writings of John Calvin; he was instrumental in having him burned in 1553

Shako—a tall cylindrical military hat made of stiff material with a short visor and a plume in front

Shamming—to pretend or feign something in order to deceive

Shandy—a drink made of beer and lemon-lime soda

Shavian split infinitive—a split infinitive is when a word or phrase comes between "to" and the "to" form of the infinitive verb (such as "to go") e.g. "to boldly go where no man has gone before" in which "boldly" splits "to" and "go"; it is a Shavian split because Bernard Shaw advocated unusual forms of expression, whereas the split infinitive is considered unconventional grammar

Shekel—money or wealth; a silver coin used in ancient Israel and the Middle East

Shelly's cloud—"The Cloud" is a poem by Shelly that personifies and gives life to a cloud as a separate living entity; figuratively, to give independent life to the objects and forces of nature

Shewbread—on the Sabbath, unleavened bread placed on a table by the sanctuary as an offering

Shift—a straight, unwaisted dress

Shikar—the hunting of game for sport

Shlemihl—an awkward or unlucky person whose endeavors usually fail

Shoat—a young pig that has just been weaned

Shoeblack—shoe shiners or boot polishers that are often young boys

Shrovetide—in Christianity, the three-day period preceding Ash Wednesday and Lent

Shuck—the husk, pod or shell of something like a pea or corn; the shell of a clam or oyster; something of little or no value

Shying—describing horses that fright easily and take a great leap sideways or bolt when provoked

Sibilant—pronounced with a hissing sound like air escaping a tire

Sibyl—a woman in ancient times thought to be an oracle or prophet; a female prophet or fortune teller

Sibylline books—a collection of closely guarded secret Roman prophecies in rhyme written in Greek

Sickle—a tool with a curved blade for cutting grass; in biology, deformed red blood cells; curved in the shape of sickle

Sieve—a device for separating wanted elements from unwanted material

Signal—something that incites somebody to action; of considerable importance, notable

Signet—a small seal, especially one set in a ring, used instead of a signature to give authentication to an official document

Sila—in Buddhism, morality or right conduct; specifically, sila consists of right speech, right action and right livelihood

Silesia—a cotton twill fabric used for pockets and linings

Silphium—a plant of the daisy family also known as laserwort or laser that was used in antiquity as seasoning and in medicine

Siluit terra—raped earth or land

Sine die—to adjourn without setting a future meeting, indefinitely adjourned

Sine ira et studio—Latin meaning without anger and fondness or without hate and zealousness; the term was coined by Roman historian Tacitus in his *Annals*

Sinecure—a job that provides a regular income but requires little work; a church office whose holder is paid but not required to do pastoral work

Sinker—in baseball, a fastball pitch with downward or horizontal movement known for inducing ground balls

Sipid—tasteful, flavorful, savory; cf. insipid

Sirloin—a prime cut of beef taken from the lower part of the ribs or upper loin; cf. loin

Sirring—present participle of sir; cf. participle

Skate—a bottom-dwelling ocean fish with a flat body; to behave in an idle or irresponsible manner

Skein—yarn wound loosely coiled together, a bundle of yarn; a tangled mass of material; a flock of wild birds flying in a line

Slate—to subject somebody to harsh criticism; a dark gray color

Slaver—to allow liquid to drip out of the mouth

Slavific—in theology, leading to salvation

Sloe-eyed—with dark, almond-shaped eyes, dark eyed

Slop chute—a chute in a ship for dumping garbage; a tavern frequented by military men

Slyph—an imaginary spirit of the air

Smatter—to study a subject or language in a lax way; to speak a language poorly

Smithy—the place where a blacksmith works

Snaffle—a bit for horses that is jointed in the middle and rings where the reins are attached

Snarky—sarcastically critical, maliciously mocking

Snood—an ornamental hairnet or fabric bag worn over the hair at the back of a woman's head; a wide ring of knitted material worn as a hood

Snook—a rude gesture of contempt by putting the thumb to the nose with the fingers outstretched

Soandso—an unnamed or unspecified person or thing, a so-and-so; a bastard

Socinian—a follower of Laelius and Fastus Socinus, Italian theologians who preached belief in God but rejected other traditional Christian doctrines

Sociophagous—existing upon or at the expense of others

Sodaine dampe—sodaine is obsolete for sudden and dampe is archaic for a feeling of gloom or melancholy, hence a sudden gloom or melancholy

Soever—in any way or to any degree possible, at all

Soi-disant—so-called or self-styled

Solecism—a mistake in grammar or syntax; something incorrect, inappropriate or inconsistent, an error; a breach of good manners; cf. solipsistic

Sol-fa—in music, the syllables do, re, me, fa, so, la and ti used to represent the tones of the scale; the use of these syllables

Solipsistic—the belief that the only thing for sure is oneself and true knowledge of anything else is impossible; cf. solecism

Solstitial—the times when the sun is furthest from the equator (about December 21) or closest (about June 21); figuratively, something that relates to two opposite points on an elliptic (like the sun at its northernmost or southernmost points relative to the equator)

Somatropsyhic—relating to the body and mind, especially with mental symptoms caused by bodily illness

Sonata—an instrumental musical composition with three or four movements in contrasting forms and keys

Sophia—an ancient Greek word for wisdom, particularly in insight, skill and intelligence, principally in philosophy and religion, from a woman named Sophia honored as a goddess

Sophistry—a method of clever argument that is flawed or dishonest; cf. casuistry

Sop—something offered as a concession to somebody who is angry or discontented; an offensive term accusing one of lack of courage

Soroptimist—professional businesswomen members of Soroptimist International that promote public service

Sororal—relating to or resembling a sister; sisterly

Sorrel—a reddish brown color ; a sharp-tasting plant used in greens and medicine

Sottish—in the habit of drinking too much alcohol; showing the effects of having drunk too much alcohol, drunk

Sotto voce—to speak under the breath or undertone usually privately and softly

Soubrette—an actress or other female performer playing a lively, flirtatious role in a play; a young woman considered flirtatious or frivolous

Sowar—an Indian cavalryman, literally "the one who rides"

Sozzle—a state of disorder; slang for to get drunk; to make wet

Sozzled—to be extremely intoxicated

Spadassin—a desperado or assassin

Spandrel—the triangular space between the exterior curves of an arch; the area between two arches and a horizontal cornice above them

Spatterdashe—a knee-length cloth or leather legging that protects clothing from water or mud that spatters

Spavin—a disorder of a horse's hock; a swelling of the hock joint in a horse

Spavined—to be in poor condition or badly deteriorated, old and worn out

Spectral—relating to a spectrum, ghostly, phantom-like, haunted, ethereal

Specular—relating to mirrors or having the characteristics of a mirror

Sphygmograph—a machine that measures blood pressure and pulse

Spicule—a small needle-shaped part, especially in sponges and corals; in astronomy, a slender column of gas that erupts and falls back

Spiel—an irritably long or glib speech, rambling, patter

Spindrift—spray that blows from the sea; driving snow or sand

Spiny—covered by many sharp, pointed parts

Spiritus mercurialis—a monstrous dragon with many transformations

Spiritus rector—a ruling or direct spirit

Splenetic—pertaining to the spleen; extremely bad-tempered, spiteful

Spoliation—the seizing of things by force, plundering

Spondee—a metrical foot of two long syllables; cf. dactyl

Spoor—the visible trail of an animal, especially one being hunted for sport

Sporti—an upper story that projects over the street

Sprat—a small edible fish of the herring family; a young, small or unimportant person

Sprighte—an elf, fairy or goblin

Sprite—an elf or fairy; a faint flash in the upper atmosphere due to the collision of high-energy electrons

Spropositi—Italian meaning blunder

Spruit—a small stream or river branch in South Africa

Squill—a plant grown from a bulb; a sea onion

Squireen—in Ireland, a rural landowner owning a small amount of land

Stadia—a method of surveying to determine distances and differences of elevation using a telescopic instrument

Staff—a fibrous plaster building material used as temporary and often decorative finish of a structure

Stasima—one of the regular choral odes between two episodes in Greek tragedy sung with the chorus standing; cf. prodos

Statu pupillari—under guardianship, especially as a pupil

Statuary—one who practices the art of making statues

Stave—long pieces of wood that when bundled together make the hull of a boat or barrel

Stave of the beadle—a stave is a staff or long piece of wood and a beadle is a lay official of a church or synagogue, thus the stave of a beadle is the staff of the lay official

Stays—in dress, a small bone, metal or plastic used to stiffen corsets, girdles and shirt collars; a corset that is stiffened with strips of whalebone, metal or other material; provides support for something

Steening—a lining of stone or brick to prevent caving in or washing away of soil

Stele—a stone or wooden slab usually taller than wide erected in the ancient world as a monument

Stella—Latin for star; a common girl's name

Sterometrical—to have a readily measurable solid form or volume

Steyned—lined, like in a well

Steyning—a small rural town in West Sussex, England; Saint Cuthmann of Steyning (b. 681 CE) was an Anglo-Saxon hermit, church builder and saint; a hermit

Sthenic—strong, vigorous or active, abounding in energy or bodily strength; cf. asthenic

Stipple—a mark with numerous small dots or specks; the process of stippling a surface, or the effect so created

Stochastic—in statistics, showing random to probabilistic behavior; involving guesswork or conjecture

Stole—a long, narrow embroidered scarf worn by the clergy; a draped robe worn by women of high rank in ancient Rome

Stolen—to move secretly, quietly or unobserved; to happen imperceptibly or gradually

Storax—a deciduous or evergreen tree with white drooping flowers in long clusters grown as ornamentals

Strabismus—to squint or to partly close the eyes, glance aside or look askance

Strangury—a medical condition caused by blockage or irritation of the bladder resulting in severe pain and the strong desire to urinate

Strappado—a form of torture in which somebody is hoisted by a rope around the wrists which are bound behind the back and then dropped and stopped before reaching the ground

Stricture—a limit or restriction, especially one that seems unfair or harsh; severe criticism or a strong critical remark; in medicine, a narrowing of a body passage

Stringcourse—a decorative feature on a building in the form of a horizontal band or molding

Stripes—a chevron sewn on a uniform to denote military rank; cf. chevron

Stroboscope—a flashing lamp for intermittent illumination

Strophe—in ancient Greek tragedy, the first part of the ode; in poetry, the first metrical form that alternates; cf. antistrophe, epode

Strumpet—an offensive term for a prostitute or sexually active woman

Stupa—a Buddhist shrine, temple or pagoda that houses a relic or marks the location of an auspicious event

Sturm and Drang—German meaning storm and stress, a German literary movement of the late eighteenth century that exalted nature, feeling and human individualism and sought to overthrow the entitlement cult of rationalism and whose prominent members included Goethe and Schiller

Stygian—relating to the Styx, the mythological Greek river that the dead were ferried across to Hades; complete darkness and frightening, like hell; eternally binding, like the promises sworn on the banks of the river Styx

Stylus—in recording, a phonograph needle that rests in the grooves of a record; a pointed instrument used in engraving, especially in ancient times for writing on wax tablets

Sub divo—Latin meaning in the open air

Sub rosa—Latin meaning happening or done in secret

Sub specie aeternitatis—Latin for viewed in relation to the eternal, from a universal perspective; God's view is sub specie aeternitatis cf. sub specie saeculi

Sub specie praeteritorum—historical thought based on the past; cf. sub specie quantitatis

Sub specie quantitatis—historical thoughts based on quantity; cf. sub specie praeteritorum

Sub specie saeculi—Latin meaning viewed in relation to the present age; cf. sub specie aeternitatis

Subdominant—the fourth note in a major scale in music; a musical key, chord or harmony based on a subdominant

Subjunctive—a grammatical mood that expresses doubts, wishes and possibilities, a way of speaking that allows people to express their attitude toward what is being said

Sublation—to deny or contradict, to negate

Sublunary—the space between the moon and Earth; belonging to the material world rather than the spiritual or intellectual worlds

Suboptimal—below the optimal level or standard

Subordinate—somebody or something lower in rank, status or class; cf. superordinate

Suborn—to persuade somebody to commit a crime or other wrong-doing; to bribe a party to lie in court

Sub-prior—in medieval times, the assistant to a prior

Succubus—in medieval times, a woman demon that has sexual intercourse with men while they sleep; cf. incubus

Suffragan—a junior bishop appointed to help a diocesan bishop

Sui generis—Latin meaning of its own kind, constituting a class alone, unique, peculiar

Sultana—a small, light brown seedless raisin used in foods such as puddings and cakes; a wife or concubine of a sultan

Sumac—a tree of the cashew family with red hairy fruit and feathery leaves; the ground dried leaves of sumac trees used in tanning and dyeing

Summum bonum—the highest good, especially in an ethical system

Sumpter—a pack animal

Sumptuary—relating to laws that limit private expenditure on food and personal items

Sunder—to separate something into parts, especially by force; to break something apart

Sundry—of various kinds, several; various items not important enough to be mentioned individually

Sunium—a cape at the southern extremity of Attica considered sacred for the gods Poseidon and Athena

Superadded—to add something onto what has already been added, to add something further

Superannuate—to retire with a pension; to reject something due to obsolescence

Superbia—Italian for pride, haughtiness, pomposity, arrogance, vanity or rudeness

Supererogation—the performance of work beyond what is required or expected, performance beyond the call of duty

Superfetation—the fertilization of a second ovum after the start of pregnancy resulting in two fetuses at different stages of development, a common occurrence in some animals

Supernal—coming from the sky; characteristic of the sky, heavenly

Supernatural—phenomena that cannot be explained by natural laws; magical; attributed to a deity

Supernumerary—somebody or something in addition to the usual number; exceeding the usual number; a substitute employee or walk-on actor

Superordinate—somebody or something of superior rank, status or class; a word whose meaning encompasses another more specific word, e.g. animal is superordinate for cat; cf. subordinate

Supinity—the quality of being supine or lying horizontally with the face or torso facing up; cf. prone

Suppurate—to produce or discharge pus as a result of an injury or infection; cf. septic, purulent

Suppurating—to discharge pus as a result of an infection or injury; to spoil

Supramundane—above and beyond the mundane; spiritual, other-worldly

Suprapersonal—psychology or psychotherapy dealing with esoteric mental experience beyond the usual limits of ego and personality

Surcease—to cease, to bring something to an end

Surplice—a white ecclesiastical outer garment like smock with wide flared sleeves

Surplusage—in law, an irrelevant matter; redundant words or arguments; an excess of something

Surrogate—somebody who acts as a replacement for somebody else; a woman who bears a child for a couple; in law, a judge who probates wills and settles estates

Surtout—a man's close-fitting overcoat like those worn by cavalry officers over uniforms in the eighteenth century

Suspicies—tending to cause or excite suspicion; questionable, suspicious behavior

Suss—to realize or grasp something; knowledge or awareness of a specific kind; to be shrewd and wary

Sutler—a civilian supply contractor

Suzerain—a ruler or nation that controls another's international affairs but allows it to control its internal affairs

Swabia—a historical region spanning Wűttemberg to Bavarian Swabia having its own unique culture and dialect

Swaddle—to wrap or bandage somebody or something with something; to wrap a baby tightly in soft material

Swain—a young man who lives in the country; a man who is somebody's admirer or lover

Swart—same as swarthy, with a dark, often weather-beaten complexion

Sword-knots—decorative ribbon or tassel on the hilt of a sword

Sybil's leaves—Sybils were women in ancient Greece believed to be oracles, Sybil's leaves are from a poem by Gerard Manley Hopkins about a Sibyl who wrote about fears of destruction and death on oak leaves

Sycophantae—in ancient Athens, informers or individuals who the populace allowed to harass and annoy the richer classes in the belief that such liberty helped to support democracy

Syllabus—a summary of a discourse, treatise or course of study or examination requirements; a list of topics or books that will be studied in a course

Symmachy—from the doctrines of the Symmachians who believed the human body was created by the devil and not God, therefore it should be subject to misuse

Synchronicity—the meaningful coincidence of psyche and a physical state or event which have no causal relationship to one another (definition from Carl Jung's *Memories, Dreams, Reflections*)

Synchrotron—an accelerator that sends particles near the speed of light in a doughnut shaped tube by magnets that produces synchrotron radiation

Syncopate—to modify a musical rhythm by shifting the accent to a weak beat of the bar; to shorten a word by removing one or more sounds or letters from the middle

Syncope—the act of fainting or a fainting fit; the shortening of a word by the loss of sounds or letters from its middle

Syncretism—the combination of different philosophic or religious beliefs; a single word that means what was previously denoted by two words

Syncrisis—the comparison of opposites

Syndic—a government official in various countries; someone appointed to represent an entity in business transactions, a business agent; in some European countries, a government official, especially a civil magistrate

Synecdoche—a figure of speech in which the word for part of something is used to mean the whole, e.g. "wheels" for "car"; cf. metonymy

Synoptic—the gospels of Matthew, Mark and Luke that tell the story of Jesus Christ's life and teachings from a similar point of view

Syringa—a lilac flower or bush; a tree with flowers like an orange tree

Systaltic—an organ like the heart that undergoes alternating rhythmic contraction and dilation, rhythmically pulsating

Systole—the contraction of the heart; cf. diastole

T

Tabasco—a hot-tasting sauce made from peppers, vinegar and spices

Table-turning—a séance where participants sit around a table, place their hands on it and wait for rotations

Tabor—a small drum, especially one used with a pipe

Taboret—a low solid seat without arms or a back

Tabula Samaragdina—also known as the Emerald Tablet, a compact and cryptic Hermetica containing secret material for alchemists

Taedium senectutis—Latin for "the tedium of old age"

Taffeta—a stiff, crisp, smooth, lustrous, plain woven fabric made from silk used in women's clothing

Tale—a number or total, as in weight and tale

Talebearing—the spreading of gossip or secrets that may cause harm or trouble

Tally—to put an identifying label or tag on something

Talma—a kind of sleeveless cloak

Talus—the bone in the ankle that connects with the lower leg bones to form the ankle joint; a sloping area of rock and rubble; the strong base of a military fortification

Tamarisk—a tree with leaves resembling scales native to Europe and Africa

Tamenusque—Latin meaning you may drive nature out with a pitchfork but she will always come back; figuratively, inborn character is ineradicable

Tam-o'-shanter—a Scottish cap with a snug headband and lose crown, sometimes having a pompom, tassel or feather in the center named after the hero in a Robert Burns poem; in the British military, a nineteenth-century traditional Scottish bonnet worn by men

Tampion—the cover for the muzzle of a gun to keep out moisture and dust

Tantalus—in Greek mythology, a king who was condemned to stand in water under a fruit tree, and whenever he tried to eat or drink, the water or fruit receded; a case for decanters of alcoholic drinks

Tantivy—a hunter's cry, especially to rouse a horse to a full gallop; a fast ride, especially on a horse; moving very fast, speedy

Taper—a piece of wood used for taking a flame to light something else; a slender candle

Taproot—a straight tapering root growing downward forming a center from which other roots spring

Tapster—a person who draws and serves alcoholic drinks at a bar

Tar—a sailor

Tare—a trailing vetch plant that has compound leaves, tendrils and bluish flowers native to Europe and North Africa; in the Bible, a weed growing among crops considered to be darnel

Tarra incognita—unknown or unexplored territory

Tarsia—another word for intarsia or an art or technique for decorating a surface with inlaid patterns, especially in wood, developed in the Renaissance

Tartar—somebody who is regarded as fearsome or ferocious; a substance consisting mostly of potassium that is deposited in wine casts during fermentation

Tartarus—in Greek mythology, the lowest part of the underworld where the worst evildoers are imprisoned; Hades or the underworld in general

Tartary—a region of eastern Europe during the Middle Ages consisting of the high plateau of central Asia and its northwestern slopes that formed part of the Tartar empire

Tartuffe—a word invented by Molière for a person who hypocritically pretends to be pious

Tautomeron—a tautomer is each of two or more isomers of a compound that exist together in equilibrium and are readily interchanged by migration of an atom group within the molecule; figuratively, an equilibrium between two groups that are readily interchangeable within a system

Tavern—a place where alcoholic beverages are sold, derived from the Latin word "tabema" meaning shed, workshop, stall or pub

Tawny—an orange-brown or yellowish-brown color

Taw—to whiten animal skins by applying alum or other mineral salts; a game of marbles

Tazia—a large, decorated paper and bamboo model of the tomb of the martyred grandsons of the prophet Muhammad paraded during the festival of Muharram

Te Deum—an early Christian hymn of praise, joy and thanksgiving also known as the Ambrosian Hymn

Teddie—a woman's undergarment combining a camisole top and panties

Teen—archaic meaning is suffering, grief; obsolete meaning is injury or harm

Teetotum—a top spun with the fingers used in a game of chance

Telesphorus—in ancient Greek mythology, a dwarf who symbolized recovery from illness; his name means accomplisher or bringer of completion

Tellus Mater—in ancient Roman religion and myth, Mother Earth, Tellus being the name of the original earth goddess in religious practices

Telyn—a harp with three parallel rows of strings

Temporize—to use delaying tactics to gain time, especially when avoiding a decision or committing oneself

Tensity—the state of being tense, tenseness

Tenter—a frame on which cloth is held taut during its manufacture

Teosinte—a tall Central American annual grass related to corn

Teratogen—an agent that interrupts the normal development of a fetus such as a virus or chemical

Tereus—in ancient Greek myth, a Thracian king

Terminus ad quem—a goal, object or course of action; a destination or purpose; a final limiting point in time

Ternary—consisting of three things or parts, arranged in groups of three, e.g. a ternary form

Terno—in gambling, a set of three winning numbers

Terrapin—a small turtle with lozenge-shaped markings on its shell found in coastal marshes of the eastern United States

Terreplein—a level space where a battery of guns is mounted

Tertian—a fever, like malaria, whose symptoms occur every other day; a tertian fever or set of symptoms

Tertium quid—Latin meaning a third party of ambiguous status, an unidentified third element in a combination with two known ones; a middle course or intermediate component

Tesserae—a small square stone or tile used to make mosaic; a bone or wood used in ancient times as a die or tally

Testimonium papertatis—Latin for "proof of poverty," also unconscious or involuntary admission of ignorance

Tetracty—a triangular enclosure comprised of ten points arranged in four descending rows, also known as a decad

Tetrahedra—plural for tetrahedron, or three dimensional geometric figures formed of four faces

Thalassocracy—a naval empire

Thanatophobia—the belief that the dead may become possessed by evil and thus become a threat to the living

Thanatos—in Greek mythology, the personification of death in Nyx, goddess of the night, the personification of death; the universal death instinct; cf. Eros

Thaumaturgy—the ability of a magician or saint to work miracles or magic, wonder working

Thaumazein—the wonder at everything

Theatrum mundi—miniature theater used to recreate current events such a military battles and natural disasters

Theism—the unrestricted belief in one God who created the world, the belief in God based on faith alone; the belief in the existence of God; cf. deism

Thelemic—a mystical religion designed to learn one's true will and achieve union; in Greek it means will

Theodicy—an argument in defense of God's goodness despite the existence of evil

Theodolite—an optical instrument consisting of a rotating telescopic sight used by surveyors to measure vertical and horizontal angles

Theodosian code—a compilation of the laws of the Roman Empire under Christian emperors and enacted by Emperor Theodosian in the late fourth century, which made Christianity the state religion of the Roman Empire

Theognis—Theognis of Megara was a sixth-century Greek poet who expounded on ethics and practical advice about life

Theogony—the account of the origin and descent of the gods

Theophanic—the appearance of a god in human form

Theoria—Greek for contemplation, looking at, gazing at, being aware of

Theosophy—the teachings of the Theosophical Society, a religious movement that incorporates Buddhist and Brahmanic theories such as reincarnation and karma

Theriac—a medical ointment concoction formulated by the ancient Greeks varying in composition used as an antidote to poison

Theriomorphic—having an animal form, especially of a deity

Thermidor—the eleventh month in the French Republican calendar named after thermal or heat

Theseus—a Greek mythical king and founder of Athens who subdued beasts

Thetic—in classical poetry, relating to stress

Theurgy—the technique of persuading a god to do something or refrain from doing something

Thew—archaic for muscle or muscular strength, as in thewy

Thraldom—the state of being under the control of another person

Thummim— one of two objects of unknown nature used for divination and worn on the breastplate of a Jewish high priest; cf. urim

Thymos—from Greek, spiritedness, associated with a physical association with breath or blood

Thyrsus—in Greek mythology a staff tipped with a pine cone carried by Dionysus

Tierce and quart—in fencing, to parry

Tiffin carrier—in South Asia, a carrier with metal containers used to carry prepared food; cf. tiffin

Tiffin—a light midday meal or snack; cf. tiffin carrier

Tilbury—a town in southeast England on the Thames River

Tilsit—a yellow semisoft cheese with mild flavor

Tilth—the condition of tilled land in terms of its cultivation history and suitability for crops; the degree of fitness of soil in the topmost layer

Tiltyard—a place where a jousting contest is held

Timbre—the quality of a speech sound that comes from its tone rather than its pitch or volume; the quality or color of the tone of an instrument or voice

Timocracy—a state where love of honor and glory is the ruling principle (Plato); a state where political and civil honors are distributed according to property (Aristotle)

Timpani—a set of kettledrums in an orchestra

Tippet—a stole or cape with long ends that hang down the front; the hanging end of a garment; in the Anglican church, a long stole worn around the shoulders of the clergy during service

Tisane—leaves or flowers used as a beverage, herbal beverage including tea

Titrate—to measure the concentration of a solution by titration; cf. titration

Titration—a way of calculating the concentration of a dissolved substance by adding measured quantities of a reagent until a reaction occurs; cf. titrate

Tittle—a tiny bit of something; a mark used in printing such as an accent or punctuation park

Toad-eater—a servile flatterer, toady, from a mountebank's assistant who would pretend to eat poisonous toads

Toddy—a drink made with alcohol, hot water, sugar and sometimes spices

Toffee—a candy made from boiling brown sugar with butter, flavoring and nuts that is soft and chewy or hard and brittle

Togue—a lake trout

Toilet—the process of attending to personal appearance and making it presentable

Toings—one of the digits of the human foot

Tom Tiddler's Ground—a child's game in which one player, "Tom," stands upon a mound while the other players try and invade his territory; figuratively, the ground or tenement of a sluggard, or one who is easily taken advantage of

Tonga—in South Asia, a light horse-drawn carriage for hire

Tonicity—the state of being tonic; a state where muscles are slightly contracted or ready to contract; cf. tonic

Tonic—relating to muscular tone or contraction

Tonsure—a shaved patch on the head of a monk; the shaving of the head, especially to shave a patch

Toper—somebody who drinks alcohol heavily and habitually

Topi—an antelope that has curved horns, a long muzzle, and bluish black and yellow markings native to Africa

Toque—a close-fitting brimless hat worn by women; a tall white hat worn by chefs; a velvet hat with narrow brim and pouched crown worn in the sixteenth century

Torque—a metal collar or armband worn by the ancient Gauls and Britons

Torsion—the twisting of something or a twisted state; a shape caused by twisting forces; the force placed on an object that has been twisted

Tortuosities—a state of being twisted or crooked; a twist or turn

Torus—an architectural term for a large convex molding, especially at the base of a classical column; in anatomy, a body part in the shape of a rounded ridge or bulge, such as the bony ridge below the elbow

Tot—a small amount of something, especially liquor

Totemism—the organization of societies into groups whose members share a common totem; the use of totems as symbols of kinship

Toto caelo—by the whole extent of the heavens

Totus—Latin for "totally thine" that expresses piety

Tournedos—a small, round cut of fillet steak

Tournure—a bustle or dress worn over the bustle

Toussaint—all saints; a common boy's name

Tout court—without qualification or additional information, briefly

Tow—fibers of flax, hemp or jute or of synthetic material such as rayon

Trabeculae—in anatomy, thin bony tissue in spongy bone that forms a mesh enclosing bone marrow; in botany, a rod-shaped cell or structure that bridges a cavity

Track—in education, to assign a course of study according to ability

Tractate—a treatise or short essay

Tralucent—same as translucent, permitting the passage of light, clear, transparent; free from disguise or falseness

Tranche—a portion of something, especially money

Transect—to cut across or to make a transverse section of; a narrow section of an object made for observation

Transept—the two parts forming the arms of the cross projecting at right angles from the nave in a church

Transference—in psychology, the transfer of unconscious feelings from one person to another; the repetition of a relationship that was in a person's childhood

Transhumant—the practice of moving livestock between different grazing lands according to the season

Transmundane—existing or extending beyond the physical world; beyond this world or worldly considerations

Transom—a transverse horizontal structural beam separating a door from a window above it; planking forming a flat surface across the stern of a ship; cf. mullion

Transuranic—an element having a higher atomic number than uranium, which is 92

Trap—a pony or horse trap is a light, often sporty two-wheeled horse-drawn carriage usually for two persons; colloquially, a mouth

Travestied—to have been represented in a false or distorted way

Travesty—a distorted or debased version of something, false representation; to imitate or ridicule something in a distorted, mocking manner

Travois—a sled with two poles connected by a frame pulled by an animal used by North American Indians

Trawl—to search through a large amount of information or many possibilities

Treacle—a thick, sticky, dark syrup made from refined sugar; molasses; cloying sentimentality or flattery; cf. treacly

Treacly—excessively sentimental; cf. treacle

Treatise—a formal written work that deals with a subject systematically and extensively

Trefoil—a three-lobed shape such as a design for an emblem used in heraldry; a plant with a part consisting of three lobes; in architecture, an ornament resembling a clover leaf

Tremolo—a wavering effect in a musical tone

Tress—a lock of long hair, especially a woman's

Trew—obsolete spelling of true, faithful, loyal

Trice—a moment, a very short time; to haul up or fasten something, especially with a rope

Trichotomous—in some beliefs, the division of human nature into body, soul and spirit; the division of something into three categories, classes or parts

Tricorne—a hat with its brim turned up on three sides worn by men in the eighteenth century; a rhetorical term with three parallel clauses, phrases or words that come in quick succession without interruption

Trill—a high-pitched warbling sound, especially made by birds; in music, a rapid alternation between two adjacent notes

Trimmer—somebody who changes their opinions or behavior to suit the circumstances in order to be accepted for personal advantage

Tripe—something absurd, untrue or worthless

Tripitaka—the discourses of Buddha collected in the first century consisting of sermons, monastic law and metaphysics

Tristan and Isolde—an 1865 romantic opera by Richard Wagner that portrays man driven by unachievable desires that only leads to misery

Tritagonist—the third actor in ancient Greek plays; cf. protagonist, deuterogamist

Triton—in Greek mythology, a god of the sea with a tail of a fish and upper body of a man

Triune—consisting of being three in one as in the Christian Trinity; a group consisting of three members

Trivet—a three-legged usually metal device used over a fire to support a pan or kettle

Troad—the historical name of the Biga peninsula in the northwestern part of Anatolia

Trocar—a steel rod sheathed with a cylindrical tube that remains after insertion used to drain fluid from a body cavity

Trochaic—relating to trochees; cf. trochee

Trochee—in metrics, one stressed syllable followed by an unstressed syllable as in the word "human"

Trod—past tense of tread; to act or behave in particular way

Trompe l'oeil—a style of painting in which things are painted in a way that makes them look like real objects, a painted representation of an object with such verisimilitude as to deceive the viewer concerning the material reality of the object

Trope—a word, phrase or expression that is used in a figurative way usually for rhetorical effect, a figure of speech; in the medieval Christian Church, a phrase or text interpolated into the service of Mass

Tropism—the turning of an organism in a particular direction in response to an external stimulus

Troth—a solemn pledge or vow, especially the marriage vow to remain faithful

Trousseau—a bride's clothes and linen, especially items that she has collected during her period of engagement

Trouvère—a medieval French poet and musician who wrote about courtly love whose works were often satirical narratives

Trowel—to apply or spread with or as if with a trowel

Troy—a system of weights used mainly in precious metals and grains with a pound of 12 ounces or 5,760 grams; cf. avoirdupois

Trull—a prostitute

Tucker—a piece of lace or linen worn around the top of a bodice or as an insert in the front of a low-cut dress

Tufa—a porous rock found near mineral springs

Tuition—the work of teaching, especially to one person, instruction, teaching, schooling, education, guidance

Tulle cap—a thin netted silk or nylon fabric used in ballet costumes, evening dresses and veils

Tumbrel—a cart used during the French Revolution to carry condemned prisoners to be executed by guillotine

Tumescence—swollen or swelling, usually due to blood or water in body tissue

Tump—to knock something over, tip over or overturn, especially accidently

Tumuli—an ancient burial mound; a barrow

Tun—a large beer or wing cask; a brewer's fermenting vat

Tunica—same as tunic, a loose wide-necked garment that extends to the hip or knee usually worn with a belt or gathered at the waist

Tunnie—same as tuna, also spelled tunny

Tupelo—the soft pale wood of a deciduous tree; a deciduous tree that grows in swamps and yields tupelo

Turbot—a European flat and circular bony fish

Turd—a person considered obnoxious or contemptible

Turmeric—a flowering plant of the ginger family

Turnspit—a roasting spit that turns; a dog formerly used in a treadmill to turn a roasting spit

Turpitude—extreme immorality or wickedness

Turve—a layer of matted earth formed by grass and plant roots; slang for peat or fuel from turve used for fuel

Tussock—a small area of grass that is thicker or longer than the grass growing around it

Twaddle—nonsensical speech or writing, nonsense

Twain—two people or things; from Kipling, "East is East, and West is West, and never the twain shall meet"

Twig—to get, catch on, realize or discern

Twit—an offensive term that insults somebody's common sense; to make fun of or criticize somebody in a playful and friendly way

Typhonic—like a typhoon, a violent tropical storm

Typology—the study of types; the study of religious texts in order to identify prophecies of later events

Tyre—an ancient Phoenician city in the eastern Mediterranean Sea in present day southern Lebanon

U

Ubiquitarian—relating to the doctrine of Luther that the body of Christ is omnipresent and therefore exists in the Eucharistic bread

Uhlan—a cavalryman armed with a lance in many European armies

Ultima ratio—the final argument; the last resort

Ultima thule—Latin for the highest degree attainable

Ultimo—in formal correspondence, the previous month, e.g. your letter of the 15th ultimo

Umbelliferous—with umbels, or shaped like an opened umbrella

Uncinate—bent like the tip of a hook, hooked

Unction—oily and thus figuratively something soothing or comforting; excessively ingratiating; pretended earnestness especially when expressed in solemn language

Uniformitarianism—in geology, the theory that changes in the Earth's crust during geological history resulted from the action of uniform processes; cf. catastrophism

Univocity—having one meaning only, unambiguous, clear-cut, definite, unequivocal

Unquent—a poison in alchemy

Unregenerate—not reforming or showing repentance, obstinately wrong or bad

Unrequite—not avenged, unavenged; not felt in response or not returned in the same way or degree, not reciprocated; cf. requite

Untermensch—German for underman, sub-man or sub-human, a term made famous by the Nazis to describe inferior people

Unum necessarium—Latin meaning one thing is necessary

Unum necesse—Latin meaning the one thing that is required

Unum vas—Latin meaning one, all one, one team, one world, always one; cf. unus lapis

Unus lapis—Latin meaning one rock, rocks, stone, one love; unum vas

Unus mundus—Latin for "one world," a concept popularized by Carl Jung under which there exists an underlying unified reality from which everything emerges and returns

Upas—a tropical tree with white bark and poisonous sap; poison made from the sap of the upas

Uprear—to rise or cause something to rise

Urdu—the official language of Pakistan

Uriah—in the Bible, the officer who allowed himself to be killed in battle so King David could marry his wife Bathsheba

Urim—one of two objects of unknown nature used for divination and worn on the breastplate of a Jewish high priest; cf. thummim

Usufruct—in law, the right to use and enjoy the profits of another person's property

V

Vade mecum—a useful book carried constantly that is referred to often; an object a person carries constantly because it is useful

Vair—squirrel fur

Valeted—to have been served by a valet or somebody employed to park a car, clean clothes or provide meals

Valetudinarian—somebody who has persistent ill health; somebody excessively concerned with their health

Vamp—a woman who uses her sexual attractiveness for the seduction and manipulation of others; to manipulate somebody by appearing to offer sexual intercourse; one who promises but does not deliver; to improvise or patch up, cobble; the front of a boot or part that carries the force of a kick

Vapid—lacking interest or liveliness, dull; lacking strength, taste or flavor, insipid

Vapors—a bout of low spirits

Variegate—to alter in appearance, especially by adding different colors; to make more varied or diverse

Varietal—relating to, characteristic of or forming a variety; made from a single specified variety of grape

Variorum—writing that has commentary by numerous scholars or editors; writing that has different versions of a text; a variorum edition contains notes written by various editors and scholars often with different versions of the readings

Vaso—a blood vessel, a vessel or duct

Vedanta—one of the six orthodox schools of Hindu philosophy that focuses on ultimate reality that leads aspirants beyond normal sense and mental awareness

Vedette—a mounted solider positioned ahead of a force to serve as a scout; a small fast boat serving as a scout for a seaborne force

Veldt—another spelling of veld, an open grassland, especially in southern Africa

Velleity—volition or desire at its weakest level, the weakest level of will

Velle—to not wish or desire; cf. nolle

Venal—open to bribery or corruption, able to be bought; characterized by corruption

Vendible—something that can be sold or be available for sale

Vend—to sell something from a vending machine; to sell something, especially on the street to make a living

Venite—the ninety-fifth Psalm from the Bible, sung as an invitation to morning prayer

Ventricles—in medicine, the set of four interconnected cavities or ventricles in the brain; cf. cisterns

Venturize—to venture, to make into a venture

Venus of Apelles—Venus Anadyomene is an iconic representation of Aphrodite made famous by painter Apelles's now lost painting

Verdigris—a bright bluish green encrusted patina formed on copper or brass by oxidation consisting of copper carbonate

Verdure—the green color associated with lush vegetation; extremely lush vegetation; figuratively a fresh, healthy or flourishing condition

Verger—a caretaker or attendant official in a church; a church officer who carries a rod before a bishop as a symbol of office

Veridical—telling the truth, truthful; corresponding to facts or reality thus genuine or real

Vermicelli—pasta in long threads

Vernier—a graduated scale used for obtaining fractional parts of subdivisions on the fixed scale of a measuring instrument such as a barometer

Verst—a Russian measure of length equal to 0.66 miles

Vesanias—mental disorders including madness, insanity and melancholia

Vesicant—a substance that causes blisters such as mustard gas used in chemical warfare

Vespers—time at about six in the evening; cf. Matins, Lauds, Prime, Compline

Vesta—in Roman mythology, the goddess of the hearth; the third brightest and largest asteroid orbiting the sun

Vetch—a leguminous plant with small flowers

Vex populi, vox dei—Latin for "the voice of the people is the voice of God," a phrase used by the radical Whigs in the early eighteenth century

Viand—an item of food, especially a tasty dish; provisions

Viaticum—in Catholicism, the Eucharist administered to the sick or a person dying and thus part of the Last Rites; provisions or money for a journey

Vicar—a wandering, unemployed musician

Vicegerent—a deputy appointed by a ruler or magistrate to authoritatively act on their behalf, especially in administrative matters

Vice-gerent—an immoral or wicked habit or characteristic; immoral conduct, depravity; criminal activity in prostitution, gambling and illegal drugs

Video meliora proboque; deteriora sequor—Latin for "I see better things (or ways) and approve, but I follow the worse thing (or way)," which describes human nature that is both strong and weak

Vili and Ve—in Norse mythology, brothers of the god Odin, who shared in creating the cosmos

Villien—a feudal peasant legally tied to a manor

Vinaigrette—a salad dressing of oil, wine vinegar and seasoning; a small ornamental bottle for holding smelling salts

Vinerian—associated with the work of Jacob Viner, as in the concept of trade diversion where trade is artificially altered causing an increased cost of imported goods; a professorship in English Law established by Charles Viner

Violoncello—Italian for cello, a large stringed instrument

Virgilian lots—a form of divination in which predictions of the future are interpreted from passages from the works of the Roman poet Virgil

Viscous—thick and sticky, reluctant to flow and difficult to stir

Vita peracta—a short written description about the life or career of a person

Viva—short for viva voce or to subject someone to an oral examination rather than written

Viver cogitare est—Latin for "to live is to think"

Vixi—Latin for "I lived"

Vizer—a high-ranking political advisor or minister

Vole—a small rodent similar to a mouse but with a shorter tail and stocky body

Voltaic—relating to Burkina-Faso or their Gur language; relating to direct electric current produced by chemical action

Volute—a spiral form or structure as in the shell of a snail; in architecture, a carved spiral decoration, often on an Ionic capital; moving in or following a spiral path

Votive—given in fulfillment of an oath or vow; showing or symbolizing a wish or desire

Voussior—a wedge-shaped element, typically stone, used in building an arch

Vulcan—in Roman mythology, the god of fire (the Greek equivalent was Hephaestus)

Vulgate—a Latin version of the Bible produced by Saint Jerome in the fourth century

Vulnerary—that which is capable of healing wounds; a drug used in healing wounds

Vulpine—typical or resembling a fox; having traits attributed to foxes

W

Wadie—a steep-sided watercourse in dry regions of North Africa in which water flows after heavy rains; an oasis

Waggery—to gossip, especially disapprovingly; a humorous or witty person

Wain—a farm wagon or cart

Walleye—a freshwater fish of North America with silvery eyes and a greenish-yellow mottled body; an eye with a light-colored iris or white or opaque cornea

Walpurgisnacht—a Germanic festival that celebrates ancestors

Wan—unhealthily pale, especially from illness or grief; suggesting ill health or unhappiness; lacking brightness, faint

Warder—warden, custodian, keeper

Watch-cockerel—a domestic young male chicken

Water-butt—a water tank

Wattle—stakes or poles interwoven with branches and twigs used for walls, fences or roofs; the loose fold of skin hanging from the throat of birds and lizards

Waylaid—to lie in wait for somebody, especially to attack or ambush; to stop or accost somebody, e.g. to waylay someone to talk to them

Wellnigh—almost, as in a mountain that is wellnigh impossible to climb; nearly, almost, practically, just about

Welter—to move in a turbulent fashion; a large number of items in no order, a confused mess

Wen—a skin cyst containing sebaceous gland material usually found on the scalp or genitals that may grow to appreciable size and become infected

Wend—to travel along a course or route

Wheedle—to coax or persuade someone to say or give something

Whey—the watery liquid that separates from the solid part of milk used in cheese making

Whiffer—a faint smell of something; a slight sign or trace of something

Whilom—former, e.g. his whilom girlfriend

Whipper-in—a huntsman's assistant who brings straying hounds back into the pack

Whippet—a fast, slender shorthaired dog similar to a greyhound bred for racing

Wight—a person of a specified kind, especially one regarded as unfortunate; a spirit, ghost or other supernatural being

Wigpated—to wear a wig, William James in *Pragmatism* referred to the "shallow wigpated age"

Winnebago—a Native American member of the Siouan people who lived in Wisconsin and Illinois; the Siouan language of the Winnebago people

Wiry—slim but muscular and strong; cf. wry

Withe—a strong, flexible twig used to bind something; to bind something with withes or strong flexible twigs or stems

Withy—a willow tree; tough and pliable, like withes; cf. withe

Woodbine—a honeysuckle climbing plant with fragrant yellow flowers, the same as Virginia creeper

Woof—a woven fabric or its texture

Woolgathering—indulging in aimless thought or dreamy imagining; absentmindedness

Wore—to diminish, weaken; to become less appealing, interesting or tolerable

Wrack—seaweed floating in the sea or growing on the shoreline, ocean vegetation; wreckage or a piece of wreckage

Writ of mandamus—an order from a court to an inferior governmental official to fulfill a specified duty

Wroth—archaic for wrathful, extremely angry

Wry—out of shape, twisted to one side; cf. wiry

Y

Yahweh—in the Bible, a Hebrew name for God from approximately 300 BCE

Yarrow—a flowering plant native to temperate regions used to feed livestock

Yasnas—the sacred liturgical texts of Avesta in Zoroastrian scriptures including the sacred hymns of Zarathustra

Yawp—a harsh hoarse cry or yelp; to shout or exclaim hoarsely

Yaws—an infectious tropical disease marked by red skin eruptions and joint pains

Yield the palm—to yield to superiority or admit defeat

Yogi—a practitioner of yoga

Ysabel—a female baby name common in France and Italy meaning consecrated to God; a unique name for females denoting one who is athletic, energetic, confident and loud

Z

Zaddik—a righteous Hassidic Jewish leader

Zion—a mountain near Jerusalem that in biblical times was emblematic of the house of God and by extension the Jewish religion; a place of Christian life and worship

Zooarchaeologist—a person who investigates animal remains from archeological sites

Zouave—a light French infantry solider with a distinct, ornamental uniform; a woman's trousers with wide tops tapering to a narrow ankle

Zymotic—relating to or producing fermentation

BOOKS BY JOHN L. BOWMAN

Reflections on Man and the Human Condition

Selected Topics in Philosophy

Nobody's Perfect

How to Succeed in Commercial Real Estate

Socialism in America

God's Lecture

A Reader's Companion

Stoicism, Enkrasia and Happiness

Aegean Summer

The Art of Volleyball Hitting

Graduate School

Provocative and Contemplative Quotations

On Law

A Reference Guide to Stoicism

A Reader's Companion II

Democracy

Philosophy and Happiness

My Travels (unpublished)

How to Get Rich

A Reader's Companion III